Free Fall
A memoir of a family
surviving the suicide of a loved one
and reclaiming life on their own terms
by
Amber Lea Easton

Mountain Moxie Publishing 2013

Although this is a memoir, a work of creative nonfiction, some of the names have been changed to protect the privacy of the individuals. This is my story, from my perspective only. Conversations and situations are from my memory and journals written during the time period involved.

Dedication

This book is dedicated to anyone who walks the lonely road of grief, who may feel alone and hopeless. My words here are meant to let you know you are not alone, that the sadness will dissipate, and that, yes, you will once again experience joy. Eventually.

Peace to you who hold this book in your hands. If you're reading these words, I can only assume that you or someone you love has been touched by tragedy and sorrow. Take care.

"Sometimes you can't let go of the past without facing it again."
-- Gail Tsukiyama, The Samurai's Garden

Foreword

On May 29, 2005, my husband committed suicide. At age thirty-seven, I was left a widow with a seven and eight-year old to raise alone. That hadn't been part of the plan. None of this had been part of the plan!

My husband had long suffered with alcoholism. He'd gone to rehab twice and was a member of AA. When he was sober, he was the most amazing man who pushed me out of my comfort zone and taught me to appreciate life on a deeper level. We had years of sobriety in our marriage, thank God. But when he wasn't sober, he was an entirely different person. Scary. Violent. Paranoid.

I'd left him several times during our ten years together, usually taking my children to hotels in the middle of the night. The last time we'd been separated, I created a story to "cover" his six-month absence while he fought for sobriety. Judge that, if you must, but I did what I did because I hoped he'd succeed. I didn't want to give up on him, on us, on the idea of happily ever after. He had a therapist, attended AA, and his recovery seemed like a reality. We shared years of happiness—dare I say contentment—before it began unraveling a year before his death.

Sean was a soccer coach, a hard worker, and a good guy whom everyone loved when they met him. He had a generous heart, an easy-going nature, and romantic soul. Each year on our wedding anniversary, he'd duplicate my wedding bouquet and surprise me with it wherever we happened to be. Kids he coached would run up and hug him when they saw him in the grocery store. No matter what turmoil brewed in our relationship, he never missed a day of telling me he loved me. There was a lot to love about the man...and a lot to fear.

So when he hung himself in our bedroom, it had to be my fault...*right?* There had to have been something I could have said or done to change the outcome...*right?*

That's what the collective jury of society decided as we remaining three Eastons struggled to piece our lives back together. Why would they think anything else? I'd covered for him and kept our secrets locked behind closed doors while I fought to keep him sober and sane for years.

In one instant—in his final act—he stripped away my identity as wife, stay-at-home mom, and best friend. In one moment our world crumbled from beneath our feet. He'd been the center of our universe but now he was gone. Everything I ever believed to be true crumbled beneath my feet.

How was I going to pay the mortgage? How was I going to maintain a mountain home alone? Would we need to move right away? Would the kids lose the only home they'd ever known? How would I explain this to the children? How could I start over while dealing with the loss of man I'd loved with all of my heart? I'd been out of the workforce for nine years—yes, that had been my choice at the time because we'd had a *plan.* Now what? What would happen to us now with our income suddenly cut by 2/3?

That's a lot to absorb. Fear. Shock. Guilt. What-ifs. Grief. Trauma. Secrets. Judgment. Uncertainty.

Being a young widow with two small children to care for created unique challenges that I was unprepared to handle. People would look at me—so young in the big scheme of things—and balk at the word "widow". Learning to say that word without cringing was a challenge in and of itself. Learning to forgive Sean, learning to find peace with the suicide, learning to let go of the identity of "wife", learning my strengths, and learning to raise two children solo without allowing their father's death to become a crutch for them—an excuse to go off the rails—has been a grueling journey.

Why tell the story, though? What's the point? My situation isn't that unique—except in my world, I know—rather, it's far too common. When this happened to me, there weren't many resources about widows of suicide raising two young children. I felt alone. Isolated. Damaged. Terrified.

I spoke with my children, who are now teenagers, and they encouraged me to write this for others who may feel alone, lost, hopeless, sad, and confused as they face their own tragedy. We never want anyone else to feel that they are somehow abnormal in their grief or that they are in any way alone.

So that's who this book is for...other widows, widowers, survivors of suicide, children, and loved ones who need encouragement that there is another side to grief. There is. We're there now. We're looking back and holding our hand out to you saying, "hang in there, you're not alone, and you'll get here, too."

The following is my unguarded truth, from my perspective, of what happened the day Sean killed himself and the subsequent days of piecing life together again. Based on journals and my memory, this is my story.

*"Some people's lives seem to flow in a narrative; mine
had many stops and starts. That's what trauma does. It
interrupts the plot. You can't process it because it doesn't fit
with what came before or what comes afterward. A friend of
mine, a soldier, put it this way. In most of our lives, most of the
time, you have a sense of what is to come. There is a steady
narrative, a feeling of "lights, camera, action" when big events
are imminent. But trauma isn't like that. It just happens, and
then life goes on. No one prepares you for it." —Jessica Stern,
Denial: A Memoir of Terror*

Chapter One
May 29, 2005

I'm sick. Last night's flight home from Cancun
was one of the worst I'd ever experienced. I started
feeling sick at the hotel before we left and it had only
gotten worse as the day continued. I'm surprised they
let me through Customs considering I'd looked like
the walking dead.

We'd arrived at Denver International late last
night from our two-week vacation in Playa Del
Carmen. For all I knew, the bags were still in the back
of the SUV. I'd pretty much collapsed into bed when
we'd gotten home.

The house is abnormally quiet. I drag myself
out of bed, feeling better but still a bit shaky. I look at
my writers' notebook that I'd tossed aside last night.
Sean had sat at the edge of the bed holding it, saying
something about me needing to read what he'd
written on the plane ride home, but I'd been sick and
exhausted so had set it aside. I glance at it now, see
that it's three pages front and back, and decide to read
it later.

Where is everyone? I finally get a glimpse of
Bree running past the window. Sean is carrying a

small aspen tree in his hands from down the hill. Ben, only seven years old, is traipsing after him through the forest carrying a kid-sized red shovel in his arms. They look like a pair on a mission.

Smoke rises from the fire pit. I'm confused. It looks like Sean and the kids have been busy with yard work all morning. I have no idea why he's outside planting trees and burning slash in the fire pit. We haven't even unpacked our suitcases from our trip to Mexico yet. Then again, I've just about given up on figuring out why Sean does what he does.

I know the end is near, I feel it. Our vacation had been an attempt to reconnect, but it had gotten bizarre with Sean's disappearances and long talks about happier days. On the flight home, he'd convinced himself that the other passengers on the plane knew we were having marital trouble, had unbuckled to sit on my lap, and accused me of telling them all of our secrets. It had scared and embarrassed me, I admit.

He either needs to return to his counselor or I'm out. I can't raise my kids in a tense household like this anymore. He needs to know this...how can he not know this? I need to tell him to get his act together or we're getting a divorce. The kids were scared of him on vacation, wouldn't let him tuck them in at night, and would shrug away from his too long hugs.

Yet now they're both trailing after him like he's their hero while I'm sleeping the day away.

I open the window and get Sean's attention. "What are you doing?"

"Transplanting trees. You said you thought these little guys would die if we didn't move them into more sunlight so that's what I'm doing," Sean says with a smile.

Yeah, I'd said that about two months ago in a passing conversation.

"Are you feeling better?" Ben asks, leaning on his small shovel as if he were manlier than his seven years.

"Yeah, I'm fine. Why don't you two take a break?" I look around the yard, amazed at all the tiny aspen trees that they'd replanted while I'd slept.

"I need to get a lot done, we'll be up in a few." Sean says.

Man, when he smiles I lose my resolve. I love him, that's the problem. My heart still flips at the sight of him, even when I'm angry or scared or worried or sick. I watch him squat down to say something to Ben and my heart aches even more. Why can't he be like this all of the time?

One minute he's normal, laidback Sean. In a blink of an eye, he's sullen, paranoid, creepy Sean. For the last year, it's been a rollercoaster ride of emotion and I'm burnt out.

I walk onto the deck for some air. I love the view from here...nothing but treetops and mountains. Peaceful. I sit on our rocking bench, close my eyes, and soak up the sun. I can't shake the nauseous feeling rolling through me.

"I think there's something living in this." Bree plops onto the cushion next to me and shoves a Conch shell into my face. "Look. It smells funny, too."

Oh, it definitely smells funky. I take the shell from her and examine it for a corpse while she bops around in front of me. Her blonde hair still in Caribbean braids bounces against her head as she dances to a song on the radio. I swear the kid has been dancing since she could stand on her own two feet.

No creature found, I set the shell down and decide to let it air out on the deck for a bit.

"We'll let it hang out here for awhile until it

gets less stinky," I say.

We're all tan from our trip. Bree, who fought against reapplying sunscreen after rolling in the waves, is sunburned. Oh well, I couldn't wrestle her down on the beach so maybe I won't win mother of the year.

I need some lemonade. I stare into the refrigerator, wishing I felt better to go grocery shopping, but that's not happening. Looks like it'll be frozen pizza for lunch.

Sean wraps his arms around me from behind and rests his chin on top of my head. I turn and we start swaying in the kitchen. Dancing randomly has always been our thing. I loop my arms around his waist and look up. He's not smiling; instead he looks confused and sad.

"Are you sure you didn't know any of those people on the plane?" he asks.

I stop dancing and turn away from him. Is he *serious*? "You know I didn't. How could I? You're being crazy. I'm so sick of this. Just when I think you're...never mind. It doesn't matter."

Just when I think he's normal...BAM...he says something insane.

"Did you read what I wrote in your writers' notebook?"

I focus on stirring the lemonade and remain silent. Something's gotta give, I know it. Not only can't I keep walking on eggshells, but the kids also deserve a peaceful home. They're young now, but soon they'll start noticing his weird mood swings and paranoia. I need to make a decision and stick to it. Maybe love isn't enough.

"I have two more trees to transplant," he says as he walks back outside with Ben at his heels.

I have no idea what's gotten into him. He's planting trees, burning slash, cleaning the yard like a madman, and now he's bringing us lemonade. He's a man on a mission, for sure, but I have no idea what's motivating his sudden urgency to get everything in order.

I lounge outside on the bench swing in the sun with my lemonade while Bree talks about what could have died in the shell. Before too long, Ben and Sean join us on the deck with lemonade.

"It's all going to be fine," Sean says, putting his hand on my knee. "I have everything figured out."

"What do you mean?" I'm hesitant to ask.

"I know I've been off, that the kids get scared of me sometimes, that you're worried that I'm drinking again. I'm not. Don't worry." Despite his smile, sadness lurks in his blue eyes. "I have it all figured out. It's going to get better. Trust me."

Both kids are investigating the shell and ignoring us.

"You need to go back to therapy, something." He's lying to me, I know it. The feeling twists my already battered stomach into knots. "What do you mean everything will be fine?"

"I have it all figured out. I'm taking care of everything."

Damn, he's a handsome man. Tall, blonde, tan, blue-eyed...his charm always tugged at my heart. I want to believe him. I don't.

"Sean, we can't keep having the same discussions over and over again. I don't know what's going on with you, but we can't keep going on like this." I put my hand on his, wishing I knew the right words to break through to him. "You were scary on the plane, something's seriously wrong."

I love this man so much. I want us to be a 'normal' family who doesn't construct lies to the outside world to hide the truth. Despite everything we've been through, he's my best friend. Even if we get divorced, I know he'll always be my best friend. I just can't keep my kids in an unpredictable environment where I never know what version of Sean I'll get when he walks through the door. Will he be happy, fun Sean? Will he be scary, paranoid Sean? Will he be distant, silent, and staring Sean? Who will he be? I can't do it. I don't believe anything he says anymore. Experience has taught me that I need to question everything. I hate living like this.

"I have it all figured out. Trust me." He squeezes my leg again, smiles that smile that's always melted my resolve and winks.

"I don't trust you, that's the problem. You need to go back to your therapist...move out maybe...until we can figure out what to do."

"Did you read what I wrote in your notebook?" He asks, his gaze more intense than usual.

"No, not yet." I think back to those three pages that I'd pushed aside. "Why? What'd you write?"

"It doesn't matter." He looks at the kids and grins. "We had a good trip, though, didn't we?"

"I suppose so." I'm hesitant to agree because of his odd disappearances and behavior on the plane ride home. I also don't want to argue. I simply don't have the energy or desire to get into it. "You need to promise me that you'll go back to therapy, that you'll call Suzanne on Tuesday."

"So you want me to go?" He nods, looks toward our mountain view and sighs. "Is that what you're saying? You're sure? You want me to go?"

"Yes, I want you to go." I think it's best, at least for a while. For months now I've woken up with him standing at the edge of the bed, staring at me in the dark. I'm not sleeping, not trusting. "Maybe the kids and I will go to South Dakota for most of the summer, stay with mom and dad, take break."

"No, I'll go. You're right. I've already thought this through. You're right." He squeezes my leg again, tight, until I look him in the eye. "You know how much I love you, don't you?"

I don't know. That's the truth. I don't. I can't help but feel that if he loved me as much as he claims that he'd be sober for good by now.

He sees the doubt in my eyes. I know he does because his entire face changes. I've never seen someone look so sad.

I don't know what to do with that sadness. We'd been on a ten-day vacation, for God's sake. I've stood by him all this time...yet there's that look and I don't know what to do anymore.

"Why are you so sad all of the time? What is it?" I put my hand over his, wanting to understand. "You need help."

"Our wedding day was the happiest day of my life, you need to believe that. I love you, Amber. You and the kids are the best thing that's happened to me in my life. I love you so much," he says with tears in his eyes.

The kids are running through the house with the dogs now. I hear them laughing, want that to stay the same. I don't know what to do. There's so much conflicting emotion in my heart.

"You need to go back to therapy," I say again. I want my Sean back, not the crazy version of him that's been around for too long.

"Do you really think I should go?" he asks again.

Now I'm getting annoyed. Same conversation with no result. How many times have we discussed him returning to therapy or to anything that could solve whatever problem I can't see? I can't do it anymore, especially not today when I feel like scorpions have taken over the inside of my stomach.

"Yes, go, I said it already. Just go. I'd better make the kids lunch, it's already mid-afternoon." I leave him sitting on the deck and walk inside to the kitchen.

From the kitchen window, I see Sean lifting the last of our bags from the back of the SUV and carrying them downstairs. He looks so sad. I'm so sick of him looking sad and not knowing how to get through to him. I don't have the right words anymore. I've said them all. I've begged, I've pleaded, I've covered for him, I've loved him, I've cried over him.

"You guys need to settle down and eat something," I say to the kids, purposely ignoring Sean's activities.

I find a game for the kids to play—dominoes—dump the pieces onto the coffee table, and curl up on the sofa behind them. A cold, sudden breeze blows through the house, hinting at the storm I see brewing over the mountain across the valley. Bree runs to close the sliding glass door leading to the deck and pulls it closed.

It's quiet. That's what I notice most. The silence filing the house while the kids eat their pizza.

"Sean," I call down the stairs, thinking he's unpacking the bags I'd seen him carry toward the back door.

No answer.

"Ben, can you go tell Daddy that lunch is ready?" I look at the clock on the mantel above the fireplace. It's 4:20 in the afternoon, not quite lunch but not dinner either. Vacation mode hasn't quite worn off yet. Time is all out of whack.

Ben lingers at the top of the stairs. "I don't want to go."

"Why?" I ask. "Just go down and tell him that the pizza is ready."

I don't want to deal with him so am sending my son in my place. Seems easier.

"I don't want to go. Something's wrong." Ben chews his fingers, looking at me from the top of the stairs.

"Okay, I'll go," I say, but Ben is already walking down the stairs anyway.

I'm once again struck by the silence of the house. Living in the mountains, it's never that noisy, true, but there's always some sound either of birds or wind or something.

No sign of Sean in the family room, the hall, the laundry room or our bedroom. The bags he'd carried had been dropped in the hall.

"Sean, lunch is ready," I call out. No answer.

"Where's Callie?" Ben asks with the attention span of a seven-year old. "We need to give her medicine."

I sigh and sit down at the edge of the bed, not really caring where the cat is. I look at the bags. Listen to the silence.

"Mom, something's wrong with dad." Ben rushes out from my closet. He tugs on my hand, urging me toward the large walk-in closet Sean had built for me when we'd first bought this house.

I don't know what I'm seeing. It looks like he's kneeling in the corner beneath his rack of clothes, my black sweater coat draped over his face, his hands hanging loose at his side.

"What are you doing?" My God, the man is redefining crazy. If this is some kind of joke, I'm going to go off on him.

He doesn't move.

Bree joins us in the closet. "Is daddy playing a game?"

"Sean, stop it." I walk toward him, not sure what I'm seeing. I push his shoulder to make him stop this stupid game.

His body swings.

I don't understand. I pull the sweater from his face. His eyes are glazed over; his tongue is sticking out sideways. There's something around his neck, tied to the rod holding his clothes, cutting into his neck. He's hung himself.

"Call 911," I order the kids while wrapping my arms around his waist and trying to lift him up. I can't think straight. Maybe if I create slack, he'll be okay. I don't know what to do. I pull at the nylon cord cutting into his neck, but it's too tight. "Sean, what have you done? What's happening?"

Bree hands me the phone.

"My husband's hung himself," I hear myself saying. My mind can't grasp what I'm seeing. I've never seen anything like this in my life.

"Mommy, what's wrong with daddy?" I hear the kids saying. I hear them crying.

I don't know what to do!

"You need to give him CPR," the 911 operators says, but I don't understand. I'm holding him, squeezing the phone between my ear and shoulder. I don't understand what she means.

"I'm holding him up, I can't. I don't understand. I don't know what you want me to do."

"Save daddy, mommy, save daddy!" Both kids are screaming and crying behind me.

"Go to the hallway," I say without letting Sean go.

"You're holding him up?" The 911 operator asks. "You need to cut him down, get him on the ground."

I can't stop staring at his face, once handsome now grotesquely distorted. Glassy eyes, tongue sticking out sideways...it looks like a mask even though I know it isn't. This has to be a joke, right? This can't be real. He's being crazy again, that's all. He's going to jump up, tell me that it's all a mistake, and then I'm going to smack him hard for freaking me out like this.

"I don't want to let him go," I say into the phone, holding him higher and tighter, trying to create slack in the noose he's made. "If I let him go, then he'll keep choking."

"You need to let him go, help is on the way, you need to cut him down and give him CPR."

I let him go, drop the phone, and race out of the room looking for a knife to cut through the black nylon cutting into his throat. The kids are in my room, crying, scared.

I cut him down. He falls to the closet floor, his 6'2 body collapsing into a heap. I grab the phone and let the operator know what I've done. I pull at the nylon cord cutting into his neck but can't get it loose. She instructs me to give CPR. I put my mouth over his, but I know...deep down I know it's not going to work. His eyes are open and glazed over. I push against his hard chest.

"Don't die on me, please don't die on me," I beg him. He's wearing his favorite shirt, the one he'd gotten on our honeymoon in Puerto Vallarta. I don't know why I'm just noticing that now but that's what strikes me. "Don't you dare leave me, leave us. Don't die on me."

I give him CPR. I follow the instructions.

"Save daddy, mommy," the kids cry.

I can't save him. I can't.

There's a sheriff behind me, telling me to go upstairs. Firemen are in the house; someone is taking the kids away from me.

I grab a fireman's arm, "bring him back to life, you can do that, right? He can't be dead, he can't be, it's not possible."

A sheriff guides me upstairs. The kids are in another room. I grab his arm. "Tell me he's not dead.

The paramedics will bring him back to life, right? Tell me he isn't dead."

He looks away from my gaze and leads me to the sofa.

Emergency personnel stream through the front door. That must be a good sign, right? Would they be here if they didn't think they could save him?

I catch the eye of a fireman. "You can save him, right? He's not dead, he can't be dead. You can save him, right?"

"There are wounds that never show on the body that are deeper and more hurtful than anything that bleeds."
—*Laurel K. Hamilton, Mistral's Kiss*

Chapter Two

I've told my story over and over to the police, to the Victim's Advocate, to the Coroner. I repeat, "made a frozen pizza, saw him unloading luggage, went downstairs, Ben looked for the cat in the closet but found his father hanging beneath my sweater." I don't know why I'm repeating this so often or why they won't let me see the kids.

I wash my face with a washcloth that someone had handed me after I'd thrown up again in the upstairs bathroom. The time frame, they keep asking about the time frame. I don't know. It'd been a lazy Sunday after arriving home from vacation, I hadn't been watching the clock.

About 30 minutes, I tell them. Maybe I'd left him alone for 30 minutes, I don't know.

Why do they care?

"Why was there a knife near his body?" The coroner asks me again.

"The 911 operator told me to cut him down," I say yet again.

"You left him hanging?"

"No, I mean yes. I'd been holding him, trying to lift him; I didn't know what to do. I didn't want to let go, she told me to cut him down. That's when I got the knife. I didn't want to let him go, I'd been holding him up, trying to create slack." I feel like a broken record.

Why won't they let me see the kids? The entire house is now filled with people in uniform. I can't count them all. It's pouring rain outside. Thunder shakes the house. I keep wiping my face with the damp washcloth.

"So how long did you leave him?" Again with the same damn question, this time from a female police officer who stood near the kitchen counter.

I snap. "However long it takes to make a fucking frozen pizza, that's how long. I wasn't watching the time."

"What was burning in the fire pit? Why would you be burning things?"

"I wasn't, Sean was. He'd been cleaning the yard." I drag the wet cloth over my face.

"Why was he burning things?"

"I don't know why he was doing anything, okay? I don't know why he was planting trees either, but he was." I'm getting frustrated. My life has been thrown into upheaval, into madness, and all these people wanted to do was discuss how long it takes to cook a frozen pizza and why there is slash burning in the goddamn fire pit.

They leave me alone, except for the Victim's Advocate named Vicky. She's holding my hand, silently being next to me, patting my back every now and then, reassuring me that the kids are fine and don't know what's happening. She tells me that she put a movie on for them in Bree's room.

In an instant, my house has become a scene from a movie. Flashing lights are outside in my driveway, strangers in uniform are moving in and out at will, someone is asking me who to call, I'm being asked inane questions, and my life doesn't feel like my own anymore.

"We should call someone to be with you, friends or family. Tell me who to call for you," Vicky says.

I tell her a few names while I grab my phone to call my parents. I call them, my friends, my family in Fort Collins...I hear myself say, "Sean's dead, he killed himself" but none of it feels real to me.

I'm standing outside in the rain because I can no longer breathe inside the house. The Victim's Advocate is at my elbow, always at my side. She's asking me questions. I see her lips moving, hear her voice, but can't understand her words anymore.

"Mrs. Easton, I need to know if he left a note of any kind," a police officer asks from behind me. I can tell he's the lead officer from the way everyone defers to him.

I think of the notebook and the pages I hadn't taken the time to read. Without answering, I walk downstairs, past more strangers, and to my bed. I purposely don't look toward my closet where I know his body still lies. I sit on the edge of the bed and grab the notebook. I read the pages now, confused. Would he have written a suicide note the night before on a plane ride home with his kids at his side? Craziness.

The words either don't make sense or I'm too freaked out to understand. He writes of the view outside the plane windows, the clouds looking peaceful. He writes that he wants to make things better for us, how he doesn't want to be an anchor holding me back. He acknowledges his sadness, our struggles, says once again that our wedding day was the happiest day of his life. He writes the Serenity Prayer. Paragraphs jump from happy to sad, handwriting changing with the mood of his words.

But he never says goodbye. He never mentions suicide.

I shake my head, drop the notebook, and leave the room without saying a word. I need to get away from all the people in the room watching my every move, analyzing our lives from the outside. I need to get away from the dead body of the man I love. I can't be here.

I go outside in the rain. I can't stop shaking. I don't know what to do or what to say or how to act.

People arrive as if in seconds, even though I know it must be hours that have passed by now.

"What do you want us to do with his wedding ring?" the coroner asks.

I don't understand the question. I understand his words, sure, but not the meaning of them or this situation. I don't want to accept this. I can't accept it. Sean is too young, too vital...this can't be happening.

"It's his ring, he keeps it," I answer.

"No, before we take the body, what do you want us to do with his ring?"

"It's his ring." Frustration is clawing against the confusion. I know what they're saying, I do. I see the coroner standing in my kitchen holding Sean's wedding ring in his hand, recognize the pity in his eyes, but I just...can't.

"Did you discuss cremation or funeral arrangements? It matters in how we handle the body...embalming...."

I blink at the guy. It's like he's speaking a foreign language. There's a policeman next to me— the same one who'd asked about a note—I grab his hand and look into his eyes. "I don't know what I'm supposed to do," I say. "Tell me what to do."

"Leave the ring on the dresser," he tells the coroner. Then he looks at me again, "Was your husband doing drugs?"

I want to throw up again. All of this is surreal. Drugs? We'd been fighting about drinking, he'd said he hadn't touched a drop of alcohol...maybe he'd been doing drugs. I don't know. I feel like an idiot. Shouldn't I know these things? I'm so naive. I've never done drugs, don't know the signs. He'd been acting nuts, yes, but I'd assumed it was alcohol. Perhaps in Sean's twisted way he'd convinced himself that he wasn't lying to me by omitting the drug use and telling me he hadn't touched alcohol in over a year.

Bastard.

Just like that, I'm simultaneously angry and sad. "He said he'd stayed sober. He'd had issues with alcohol, but I'm not aware of drug use. So that's it then? Was he on drugs? Did you find something?"

They all look at each other but no one answers me. That's when I see the pity in their eyes. They avert their gazes, mutter things I no longer listen to while I absorb the facts. My husband killed himself. He'd been that sad and I hadn't known. He'd been on drugs and I hadn't known. He'd hung himself in the room directly beneath the kitchen where I'd baked a fucking frozen pizza while his little children had played dominoes. Had he heard our voices through the floor while he slipped the nylon cord around his neck?

I hadn't wanted to know. I'd wanted to believe that he'd stayed sober. I'd wanted to believe that a therapist could cure his sadness. I'd wanted to believe all things were fixable, now everything I knew to be real seemed like a lie.

"If it's any consolation, it's my experience that people who cover themselves are conscious that they'll be found by a loved one and are trying to protect that person by hiding themselves. That's probably why he covered himself with your sweater...he was trying to protect whomever found him," the policeman whose hand I'm gripping says.

Consolation? Seriously? Protect me? What the hell? I stand up from the table and look—really look—at each of the people gathered in my house.

"Did you find something? Is that it? Was he on drugs?"

No one answers me. I suddenly notice the notebook in a policeman's arms. I stare at it, guilt consuming me. What if I'd read it last night or this morning? No, the words didn't make sense, but Sean had asked me if I'd read it and I hadn't. Would it have made a difference? I can't stop staring at it.

"That's my writers' journal. Why do you have it?"

They all look at each other. "It's evidence," someone says.

"Evidence?"

"Of his unstable thinking," the lead policeman says. "We need to take it."

Evidence? I'd ignored it, set it aside...he'd written about clouds, for God's sake, and that was evidence that he'd been suicidal?

"I didn't read it, I didn't know." I feel I need to explain.

Again with the pity in their eyes. I can't stand looking at them.

"If I'd known, I would have stopped him. I tried to save him." I rub my face, longing for clarity. "I tried to save him, I did, I couldn't. I wanted to save him."

I'm not sure if I'm talking about today or the past ten years.

"About cremation or burial, Mrs. Easton...what would you like to do?"

Oh. My. God. I don't have the answers.

"Cremation," I hear myself say. We'd talked about it once, after my grandfather's funeral a few years ago. It had seemed like a casual conversation about what-ifs...now it all came into my mind in vivid detail.

"We need to take the body now. Would you like to say goodbye?"

Has everyone gone crazy? Would I like to say goodbye? My entire body is shaking. I know I'm supposed to know the answers, that I'm somehow supposed to know what to do, but I don't.

"His mother isn't here yet, she'd want to see him," I say.

"She said she was feeding her horses, that there was nothing for her to do anyway, and would be here later," the Victim's Advocate Vicky says to me.

Feeding horses? Sure. Whatever. The entire universe has flipped upside down, that's the only explanation for what's happening.

I look around the room. Police officers stand in my living room. Lightening flashes outside. People are there—my aunt, cousins, friends—but I don't remember them arriving. My kids are laughing in the center of the room; my daughter's wearing a feather boa and performing for the guests.

It's an insane scene. Maybe *I'm* on drugs because nothing about this makes any sense. My husband is dead. How can that be possible? He is too young, only thirty-four, too vital, too gorgeous, too devoted to his family...*right?*

Wrong. Everything I thought is wrong.

My cousin takes my hand and we go downstairs together. Sean's on a stretcher in the middle of the family room. His blue eyes are staring unseeing at the ceiling. Weren't they supposed to close his eyes for him? That's what they do in the movies. His eyes are open and that seems wrong to me.

I touch his chest, hard and muscular, covered in his favorite T-shirt from Senor Frogs in Puerto Vallarta. I hug him, not sure what to say. I hold tight, not caring about the people watching.

His last words about making sure everything would be okay, that he'd go...all of it took on new meaning now. I'd told him to go...but I hadn't meant this.

I smooth my fingers over his blond hair and trace the bones of his face, so handsome and tan. I want him to wake up. I want this to be a fucking

nightmare or a sick joke—maybe I'm the one who
needs to wake up. I touch his hands, his long fingers.
He feels like Sean...shouldn't he feel different?

What words do I use to say goodbye to the man
who was my best friend, the father of my children?
We'd fought, we'd loved, we'd laughed, we'd cried.
Yes, it had been a hard road, but we'd been traveling
it together.

"I love you," I say against his ear.

That's all I know to say.

"Shock is a merciful condition. It allows you to get through disaster with a necessary distance between you and your feelings."
--*Lisa Kleypas, Sugar Daddy*

Chapter Three

I'm looking at urns at the funeral home. *Urns!* Who knew they came in so many choices? There are pamphlets and samples. People are asking me questions about music and programs and guest books and obituaries. I've never planned a funeral before. I'm only thirty-seven, was thirty-six just a month ago. I'm too young to be a widow, that's all I can think.

My hands shake over the examples of poems I'm supposed to choose from for the inside of the funeral program.

"I can't do this." I lay my head on the table. It's not that I can't do it; every fiber of my being rejects doing it.

This isn't supposed to be happening, not in my life, not in my children's lives, not to Sean who was such a vital, vivid human being.

"You can do this," my friend Jo says as she rubs my back. "You can, I know you can."

I think she's wrong.

My dad rubs my arm. "You can do this."

Why do I *need* to do this? Only a few days ago Sean had been teaching Bree to boogie board in the Caribbean. A week ago we'd been on a boat to Cozumel, soaking up the sun and being a fun family of four. Why do I need to be picking out urns and flowers and programs and hymns?

I'm the widow...Sean's widow. A surge of protectiveness rushes through me. He is more than how he died, I need to be strong for him, make sure people know he was better than his ending.

I choose a poem about rivers and the

mountains because he loved nature. The picture looks like the rivers near our home. Fitting, I suppose. I pick out two urns—small ones for the kids so they can take a piece of their father with them wherever they go in life. They're gold and pearl covered urns that look old, like a Mayan artifact that reminds me of our many trips to the Caribbean and Central America. I choose those, everyone nods and smiles their reassurance.

I'm doing it. I'm functioning like a human being.

I don't want to be doing any of these things...I want to be curled up, crying in the dark alone. I feel like my heart has been ripped out. I can't stop shaking.

"We need to shop for funeral clothes for the kids," someone says.

"Who's going to do the music at the church?" someone else asks.

"We need to get those braids out of Bree's hair," another comment.

I hear them all, but can't figure out why they're all so normal. The world has just split in two and we're going shopping.

I feel like I'm pretending to be a whole person. I slump in the chair, feeling defeated with talk about obituaries and death certificates.

"You're not the only person who's ever lost a spouse," another person says.

I wonder if these comments are meant to be supportive or to "put me in my place". My husband died—a first for me. Can't I have a moment to let that sink in, to cry, to fall apart?

I know I need to be strong for the kids' sake, but I'm not sure what that means in the big scheme of things. Isn't it okay for the kids to see me cry over the loss of their father? Isn't it okay that I don't want to go shopping or make small talk or laugh? What does being strong mean in the face of this enormous loss?

I'm not a fool. I know I'm not the first person in human history to lose a spouse, to be left to raise children solo. I understand that people do it all of the time across the world—but *I've* never done it. Even on the first day of a new job, a person is given some slack. That's what I need. Slack. I lost the man I loved, the man I'd intended to grow old with, the man I'd given up a lot for—he's gone as if he'd never been.

Does that make me weak--this need to fall apart, even if only for a few hours? Does that make me somehow less than because I don't know all the answers? Is it really so wrong that I crave a reprieve from the madness?

Everything inside me rejects this reality. Sean was too young to die, especially like this. That's the thing right there—suicide. The word no one wants to say out loud. Suicide. It's like a flashing neon sign over my head. For some reason, this invalidates my grief to those around me. I hear things like, "you're so lucky he didn't kill all of you, that happens all the time in the news"..."you'll be better off in the long run if he was that sad"..."he's so selfish, so cruel"..."killing himself in your bedroom was like a giant fuck you to you and the kids, he knew you'd find him." All of the comments make me sick.

I need silence, but all around me people are chattering with each other and on their cell phones. All I want is some peace.

He's been dead two days. That's it. I shut out the comments, no longer ask for silence because no one around me is 'getting it.' All I want is time alone, to figure out what happened and why.

But we go shopping and stick to the to-do list. I put on the strong facade while inside my heart's been shattered. I'm like Humpty Dumpty who fell off the wall...and no one can put me back together again.

"Only people who are capable of loving strongly can also suffer great sorrow, but this same necessity of loving serves to counteract their grief and heals them."-- Leo Tolstoy

Chapter Four

I need a break from the nuttiness so I take Jo with me to go the swimming pool where Bree is supposed to be at swim team practice. It feels like a 'to do' item on an ever increasing list, but I need to go, tell the coach what happened, explain Bree's absence, feel like I'm still in control of my life.

"What do you want me to do about it?" the coach asks.

Reality really does suck. I stare at the coach, a woman about fifteen years older than me, and absorb her response for a minute. I just told her that Bree wouldn't be at practice this week because her dad died and she says this to me? It's not like I wanted her to break into tears and hug me, or anything like that, but I thought perhaps an "I'm sorry to hear that" or something. She also knew Sean. I don't know anymore what to expect and, quite frankly, don't have the energy to think about it further. Should I not have come? I don't know. I couldn't find her phone number and am holding the tattered pieces of my life together as best as I can.

I walk back to the car feeling foolish and out of sorts. A week ago I always knew what to do...I juggled everything, had no problem making a decision...now I feel like any decision I make is wrong, even something as simple as letting a swim coach know my daughter won't be at practice feels uncomfortable.

"She's a piece of work," Jo says once we're back in my car.

"No one knows what to say." I realize that I'm expecting something that doesn't exist: understanding.

How can someone else understand this situation when I, the person living it, don't have a clue?

I drive past the exit to my house and continue down the mountain. I'm simply not ready to dive back into the fray.

Red Rocks Amphitheater has always been my safe haven. Countless concerts on summer nights...good memories here. Peaceful energy. I take Jo into the amphitheater, but sit on a bench a few feet away from her to simply breathe.

Runners jog up the stairs, a few tourists snap photos of the stage below, the sun shines brightly over Denver...life goes on like normal as if the world didn't just end Sunday night.

I watch the activity around me, feeling hollowed out. I want to stand up on the stage and shout, *"My husband died! Stop everything! How can the sun be shining? How can people be laughing? Stop laughing! I'm bleeding to death here...I'm shattered. Help me. Please help me."*

I remain seated, stay silent, hear the voices around me, feel the breeze on my face, and think about all the love I have for Sean. I love him. I want a do over on that last day. I want him to tell me the truth about what was going on in his head. I want to read his note and actually understand what he meant by it. I want...impossible and magical things.

I lose track of time. My cell phone is ringing, people are texting, but I don't want to leave this place. I don't want to deal with the business of death.

Jo and I go out for margaritas...let the avoidance begin! To Jo's credit, she keeps me on task with the list for funeral arrangements and it's much easier to handle on a patio bar with some tequila.

I'd asked Sean's family—his mother and relatives from San Diego—what they wanted to do about the obituary or the funeral, but they aren't much help. I know they're coming over to the house later today. It's so unreal, all of this. That's all I can think about, how none of this feels like reality.

I've been blindsided, yet people assume I'll know what to do. Why would I know? Nothing in life has prepared me for this moment in time, for these circumstances.

I get a text asking about the soccer team party tonight and cringe. Sean had been coaching the team since Ben was in preschool. The end of season team party is tonight and people want to know what to do about it.

Another decision.

I order a second margarita and soak up the sun a few minutes longer.

"Let the kids go to the party, but have someone else handle everything. You don't need to go," Jo suggests. "Ben should have his party."

I feel like I'm truly in CrazyLand. His dad has just died, but I'm supposed to make him go to the party? People already talked me into sending him to school today as if nothing had happened so that I could take care of arrangements alone.

My head wants to explode. I'm torn because I want help, that's true, but some of this seems absurd. Or maybe I can't think straight and it's all normal. I don't know. I'm starting not to trust myself.

Another voicemail asking me what I want to do with the soccer team next year because people need to register—Sean hasn't even been dead two days yet. His employer leaves a message wanting to know when they can come and get the company truck.

I want to scream at the top of my lungs: *"Stop! My husband just died! I need time to think!"*

Even though I'd rather stay at the bar, have more margaritas, and shut out the world, we leave.

The scene at home hasn't calmed down. More relatives have shown up. Sean's biological father comes with the San Diego relatives. Sean hadn't spoken to the man in three years, but here he is looking devastated and hostile.

I put on my best hostess face as he approaches me.

"Who cares? I care," he says.

I have no idea what he's talking about. Not once did I say that he didn't or wouldn't care. I'm not sure where this is coming from and don't have the energy to worry about it.

Those are the only words the man says to me.

Someone picked the kids up from school. My mother-in-law brings Christmas presents into the living room. It's June. She's held onto these presents for over five months—essentially holding them hostage because of a disagreement she'd had with Sean about a dog—but feels today is the right moment to deliver them. My living room becomes center stage as people gather around to watch the kids open gifts. My mother in law hands me one that's labeled "Sean and Amber". I open it...it's a blanket with a note that says, "for snuggling on cold nights" and a popcorn maker.

My husband is dead! Again, I'm fighting the urge to scream at these people gathered in my home, drinking beer, whispering in corners, and watching me expectantly.

What am I supposed to say to a Christmas gift given in June intended for my deceased husband and me? This all must be a joke, a twisted, really fucked up joke.

"Can I have a tour?" Sean's uncle asks. We've lived in this house for eight years, he's never once visited, and now of all days he wants me to give him a tour of the place.

CrazyLand. I'm telling you...I've become the mayor of CrazyLand.

"I wore your promise on my finger for one year
I'll wear your name on my heart til I die
Because you were my boy, you were my only boy forever."
-- Coco J. Ginger

Chapter Five

It's the day of the funeral. I didn't sleep at all last night. The kids won't let me out of their sight so they slept in my bed, which is fine. I stayed up writing all night, trying to get my eulogy right. I must protect Sean, that's all I can think. Everyone has their ideas of him and his death, I've already heard the claims. "How selfish of him, how cowardly." Well, today is not a day for that. I won't have it. I'm determined to stick up for him. That's my job as his wife, his widow. I must protect him...like I did in life, I suppose. I can't help feeling like I failed at that given where I am at the moment.

I crumble to my knees in my closet, the same place he died. I hold my black dress to my body. Despair ravages through me. Raw. Unyielding.

"How could you leave me?" I ask the place on the tile where I'd given him CPR. "How could you leave us? I don't know what to do or what to say or where to begin or how to do any of this alone. I am so mad at you, do you hear me?"

I curl up with my dress in my arms and sob. I want him back. I want this all to be a nightmare. Silent, body curling sobs roll through me.

"I love you so much," I manage to say against my fist. "I'm so sorry I didn't save you."

Jo appears out of nowhere and grabs my shoulders, "It's going to be okay. You can do this."

"I don't know how to do this."

"You do. Come on. You can do this." She pulls me up. "One day you'll realize that you're better off."

No one knows what to say to me. No one knows the right words.

I get dressed like a zombie, not caring about how I look.

The funeral home is on the phone, my mom says. I need to pull it together, handle things.

"Your father-in-law is requesting half of Sean's ashes," the woman on the phone tells me.

Half of *what?* My hands shake on the phone. The idea of splitting Sean's body up like that even more...the fact that the man hadn't had the respect of asking me directly or even to give me his condolences the other day...and there's that bit about him not speaking to his son for the past three years.

"He has no right to them," the woman continues when I remain silent. "You're the widow, you paid for this service. He has no right to them unless you give me permission."

"No," I say.

CrazyLand, USA, I swear.

The term "stranger than fiction" enters my mind while I convey the story to my family as we get ready to leave for the church. I'm scared of going to the church, actually. I don't expect anyone to be there. Sean and I were each other's best friends so our social circle was limited. We did everything together. It's the last day of school so I don't expect any of the soccer parents to be there. What a shame, an empty church for a wonderful man.

But people *are* at the church. Jo and my family had put together a picture collage of Sean. One of the photos had been taken exactly one week ago while we'd been snorkeling in Playa Del Carmen, Mexico, as a family of four. I squeeze the kids' hands a bit tighter and we walk to the front pew. I don't want to greet people or talk yet, not until I give the eulogy. My entire body is shaking. I don't want to be here. I want to be back in Mexico with my gorgeous husband walking on the sand.

The music, the hymns that I chose, all are happening around me. I go through the motions. Sit. Stand. Sing.

Then it's time for me to talk about him—my moment to make sure everyone knows he is more than a man who committed suicide. That's when I look up and see the people who've shown up for us. The entire back two pews are full of men who worked for Sean—they're crying. I see my cousins, my brother, and my parents, all who've traveled a great distance to be here. I see friends. I see Sean's side of the family; his mother bent over in tears, his stepfather and biological father, relatives from California. All are looking at me.

I don't know if I have the strength to speak. What was I thinking? I glance at my pastor who has tears in her eyes.

Then I feel as if I'm being held up—I feel a presence at my side, holding my arm, keeping me from falling. I look at my two little kids and speak.

I tell the room of a man who dragged us outside in the middle of the night to watch meteor showers, who loved the ocean and mountains, who loved his family, who enjoyed his job working outside every day. I tell them all how he taught his daughter to boogie board, both kids to ski before they could walk, and how he taught me to push past my comfort zone. I speak only of the man I loved.

I never take my gaze from my kids' faces. I do this for them. I want them to remember my words. I want them to remember their father for who he was, not how he died.

I hope he's here, actually. I hope Sean is here in spirit, watching us, helping us.

When it's over, I sit. I see his uncle approach the podium where he tells a story about Sean as a teenager wanting to visit his grandmother in San Diego. But Sean didn't have any money or people who would help him get there, so he rode a skateboard from Colorado to California just so he could be at his grandmothers' birthday.

I'm not sure if this speaks more to how determined my husband could be or to how alone he'd been in the world. I wonder if he felt alone all of his life, despite the love the kids and I had for him. All of this wondering and trying to be strong is taking a toll on me. I'm not sure I can keep going. All I want to do is sleep...cry and sleep. But that's not an option.

We leave the funeral home, a long convoy of people headed to the mountain where we're scattering his ashes. My pastor leads the way wearing her red cowboy boots. I hold the urn as I hike up the hill where we walked many times as a couple and then with toddlers in tow. With every step, I feel him with me, even if it's only a fantasy. I think of his smile, the warmth of his touch, his laugh, and his big blue eyes. I miss him so much I can barely breathe.

We walk to the top of the mountain. The view is brilliant from this spot. We can see the river far below and the higher mountains in the distance. A hawk flies close. It's peaceful; a place where we'd picnicked as a family.

It's a small group here, only close friends and family. We each take a turn saying a few words before helping scatter the ashes over the side of the mountain. His aunt sings, "you are my sunshine, my only sunshine" and does a little dance. I'm last to hold the urn, the one to toss the final amount of ashes to the wind. All I say is, "I'll always love you."

I may never understand why this happened. When someone is as loved as this, how can they feel desperate enough to kill themselves? Did I not do enough? Why couldn't he fight?

I wait until everyone else leaves the boulders, needing my last minutes with him. I know that when I walk down the mountain, I will do so only as a widow, no longer a wife. I feel such a sense of loss, of sorrow, confusion, and anger. Why? I never realized I could detest a word as much as 'why'.

During the funeral, my pastor said some wise words about Sean's struggle for sobriety. She said, "sometimes even the strongest of people get tired, sometimes no matter how well they're loved, they're simply overcome with weariness." Perhaps Sean had simply become exhausted with the fight, I will never know. The answers are with him...in the wind...lost to me.

Acceptance is a scary concept. How can I accept this when only a few days ago we'd been together? If I accept this, won't I be saying it's okay? Because it isn't okay, not even a little bit.

This wasn't part of the plan. Even if things were rocky, we made it work somehow. Even if we'd ended up divorced, we would have remained best friends. There are very few people in this world that can fit the word 'soul mate', but that's what Sean is—was— for me. My soul mate, my plus one, my best friend, my lover, my confidante, my biggest fan, my partner, my thorn in my side...my husband.

This isn't fair. I want one last argument, a real showdown where I'd tell him to get it together, damn it. I want one last time of holding on to him, kissing him, reassuring him that I love him. But all of that's over now. I will never get one more anything with him.

As I sit here alone, I think of the kids and I'm afraid. How can I do it alone? I gave up my career to stay home, moved to the mountains, but now what?

Am I supposed to give up the house now, too? Are the kids' lives going to be thrown into more turmoil? Am I supposed to go back to work full time, give up writing, leave Colorado? What do I tell them when they ask why their dad left us? What do I say when they graduate high school or get married or have their first child? Nothing in life has prepared me for this moment or for these decisions. So many questions that have no answers.

A week ago we'd been snorkeling in the Caribbean. I remember looking at him walking along the beach with the sun reflecting on his blond hair, him laughing at the kids playing in the sand, his muscled body still taking my breath away even after ten years together. Seven days later he's been reduced to ashes blowing down a mountainside.

How do I accept that?

As I walk down the trail clutching the empty urn to my chest, I start laughing. Sean would think it was hilarious that I had all those San Diego relatives traipsing up this mountain trail in their dress shoes. I picture him smiling at me, giving me a wink like he always did, and somehow that lifts some of the sorrow from my shoulders. At least for now.

"Hey, I warned them to bring appropriate shoes if they wanted to come up here," I say to myself.

I can hear his laugh in my memory and know he'd approve.

Chaos greets me back at the house. People arrived early and are in the house waiting for me to...do whatever it is I'm supposed to do as a widow. Does that mean hostess? I'm so tired, don't want to make small talk, but I smile and answer questions like a robot.

"Did you have life insurance?" A woman I barely know asks.

"Are you going to sell the house?" *I've heard this question a thousand times in the past few days.*

"What about the soccer team? Registration for next season is coming up, will you take it over or do we need to find someone else?" *Seriously?*

"Were you guys fighting when it happened? Couldn't you stop him?" *I feel like I'm going to throw up.*

"Are you getting the kids in counseling? You need to do that right away or they'll be messed up for their entire lives." *Gee, thanks, one more thing on my to do list.*

"Suicide is the ultimate rejection," his mother says to me, blame in her eyes. *I think of his words about how much he loved me and struggle to reconcile that with his final act in life.*

I hear everyone discussing my financial situation as if I'm not in the room, hear them talking about how Sean was our main source of income, that I could never support the family as a freelance writer, that I'd have no choice but to sell everything.

None of this comforts me.

I hear people talking about how selfish Sean was for committing suicide, how I should lie when people ask me how he died, how lucky I am that he didn't kill us all if he was that depressed.

All of that makes me want to protect him. Again. Always.

I see people going through our photo albums, passing them around, laughing at the stories. I see the kids racing around with their friends who've come to visit as if they have no idea that their daddy is never coming home. I see people invading my house from the deck to my bedroom where he died—checking out the scene as if it were a tourist destination.

I shouldn't have had the reception here, but the church had been booked that afternoon and I'd thought it would be best for the kids to be home. I've never planned a funeral before, didn't know what's right or best. So here they all are, my house open to all who cared to come. And they kept coming, although I didn't believe they would. Cars are lined up down the block.

Everyone's talking to me, but I can barely understand the words coming from their mouths. I'm so tired, but I'm still standing and talking.

"You handled this with grace," Brian from San Diego says to me before leaving.

I don't feel very graceful, but I thank him anyway.

When I finally sneak away, I hear an inner voice-like a whisper—telling me that it's all going to be okay, that we'll make it, that I know what to do, that I'm strong enough, that Sean believed I could do anything.

I doubt it.

That night, after all the guests had left, the kids and I curl up in my bed with me in the middle. I wrap my arms around them, the reality sinking in that it really is just the three of us now. I'm so afraid.

Finally, the sobs come while the children sleep.

"Grief is like sinking, like being buried. I am in water
the tawny color of kicked-up dirt. Every breath is full of
choking. There is nothing to hold on to, no sides, no way to
claw myself up. There is nothing to do but let go.

Let go. Feel the weight all around you, feel the squeezing
of your lungs, the slow, low pressure. Let yourself go deeper.
There is nothing but bottom. There is nothing but the taste of
metal, and the echoes of old things, and days that look like
darkness."
-- Lauren Oliver, Pandemonium

Chapter Six

Keep the routine, keep moving. That's what I'm
thinking as I load the car for a weekend swim meet
about 3 hours from home. Sean's funeral was
yesterday, yet here we are going to the swim meet
today.

The kids are little and don't understand the
enormity of their life change. Maybe I don't either,
not fully. All I can do is keep the forward
momentum going...so we're headed to the swim meet.

My brother is staying through the weekend. He
and mom are coming with us to Gunnison.

As I drive through the mountains, I feel almost
manic. Tunes are up. I'm singing. The kids are
laughing in the backseat.

Sean's funeral was yesterday.

Keep moving, don't stop.

My hands are shaking on the steering wheel, but
I ignore it. I don't have time to fall apart, not with
two little kids depending on me. People seem to be
supporting my decisions so far...the swim coach
wants Bree at the meet, everyone told me that this
was best for them, better than sitting around at the
house feeling sorry for ourselves.

The thing is that I *do* feel sorry for us. Our
world revolved around Sean, for better or worse. I'd
given up a good career to stay home with the kids, to
work for 'fun money', now what? I'm not a stay at
home mom anymore, yet here I am acting like it.

Smile for everyone, make them feel
comfortable, go through the motions of the living...I
can't stop shaking.

At the swim meet, Bree excels at the 100
Freestyle—out laps everyone in the pool. I watch,
sort of awestruck at this 8-year-old girl as she touches
the wall a full lap ahead of her opponents. Her entire
team is cheering for her on the sidelines, standing in
the bleachers and calling her name.

Swim coach comes up to me, squeezes my arm,
and says, "I think her dad was pushing her on."

Don't cry, not here, I think as I nod.

"I'm going to try to get back here a lot, be a
part of the kids' lives," my brother says as we sit in
the pool area. "Have you thought about making a
will? You're all they've got now, there should be a
plan in place."

We'd already agreed he'd be the guardian should
something happen to me, but I'm so sick of talking
about Sean's death as if it's simply a business deal
gone wrong that I need to correct.

Call a lawyer, make a will...another thing on the
to-do list.

I want to throw up. It seems like I haven't been
well since a week ago during our trip to Mexico. I
can't sleep, can barely think, can't stop shaking; yet
here I am at a swim meet watching my daughter
qualify for state, hearing everyone cheering her on,
making plans for guardianship poolside, and smiling
at everyone's condolences.

Maybe this really is CrazyLand. Maybe I died
and this is my Hell. None of it seems real. No one

wants me to cry, everyone expects me to be so strong for the kids. But what does that mean, that word 'strong'? I'm sick of hearing it and have no idea why so much is expected of me.

Yes, I know the importance of stabilizing life for the kids' sake. They've been my number one priority since the day they were born. That's why I quit my job to stay home, after all. They've been the center of my world and they're great kids. I'm not just saying that either, they really are nice little human beings. I want to keep them that way, am scared to death Sean's suicide will derail their lives in ways I don't yet foresee.

That sums up how I feel, actually...scared to death.

Even as I sit here with the swim team people applauding my daughter's success, I'm terrified that I am making the wrong decisions. Should we have kept the plan to come here, to get away from the house only a day after the funeral? I know everyone says that this is good, but it doesn't feel right.

What do I know? Maybe nothing will feel right ever again.

A week ago we were still in Playa Del Carmen, a family of four, shopping. He'd even looked at a new wedding ring for himself because his had gotten beaten up. Why would he do that if he knew he was going to kill himself a few days later?

Within the past seven days, I'd gone from wife to widow with zero time to comprehend it all. Just thinking about it makes my head hurt. So I don't think. I smile on cue, put one foot in front of the other, worry about snacks for the kids, and make sure Bree has dry towels after each event. I'm like a robot, a hollowed out machine that performs tasks on command without thinking.

"We're going up to Crested Butte, can Bree come with us?" a swim team mom asks.

I hear myself agreeing, see Bree smiling, and just go with it. She's only eight years old, I remind myself. She needs this normalcy, the routine. She'll have her whole life to cope with the enormity of her dad's final decision in life.

My cell phone rings. Caller ID says it's from my house, yet no one is supposed to be there. I pick it up. Static. I ask if this is my cousin, thinking perhaps she'd forgotten something there and had used the spare key. Still static. I hang up, a strange feeling coming over me. I stare at the return number, not really trusting myself anymore. Home. No one's home, though.

My first thought is that it's Sean and that he's confused. That's impossible, though. I don't believe in ghosts. My second thought is that I've lost my mind, which seems more probable.

"Someone just called from my home number," I tell my brother.

He shrugs it off as a fluke.

Maybe it is. It must be.

* * * *

Three weeks later, we're finally alone as the Easton Three. I'd been craving silence, time to ourselves, but now it's sinking in. This is our new normal. I call therapists, make arrangements for the kids to see a children's grief therapist, make an appointment for me to see someone, too. It's only been weeks since his death, but I've learned one thing: no one around me is equipped to deal with this situation so I need professional support.

Someone was in our shed while we were gone over the weekend. Tools are missing. Sean had been in construction and the shed had been his domain so I'm not sure what's gone, but know there is a

significant amount missing. I learn that some people
from his work came by to get his company
truck...they must have taken some of his tools, too.

In the shower, the water goes off while I'm
washing my hair. This has been happening since Sean
died. I've replaced the well fuses twice in only a few
days. At first, I thought it was because our house was
full of people and we were overloading the system.
But it's only us here now. Wrapped in a towel, I
traipse out to see what's going on. Another fuse
blown.

"Why don't we have water?" Bree asks from
behind me.

"The fuse keeps blowing," I say, feeling as
frustrated as she looks.

"Nothing works since daddy left," she says, her
eyes welling up with tears. "You should have saved
him."

I stop what I'm doing and stare at her despite
the soap sliding into my eyes. There it is: blame. I'd
seen it in his mother's eyes, heard it in his father's
voice, but I hadn't expected it from my children.

"We're going to lose everything now, aren't
we?" She shouts at me, her face red and tears
streaming down her face. "We don't even have
water!"

"I can fix the water—"

"You can't do anything! We don't have anything
now that daddy's gone. Nothing works. We're going
to lose everything. I heard people saying it; everyone
said we're going to lose everything now. We don't
even have water!"

I grab her and hold on tight as she sobs. Finally.
Tears.

"I can do this, it's going to be okay," I say
through my own tears.

"You can't, you can't do anything," she shouts with a stomp of her foot.

She's only eight, I know, but her words rip me to shreds. Defeat whispers through my mind. She's right...I didn't save Sean, I have no idea what to do next with my life, the water keeps going off, and I'm standing in the hallway wrapped in a towel with soap running down my face.

Right then and there I swear I won't let my kids down. Somehow we'll pull through. How? I have no idea.

I rock her until she's quiet.

I wish I could think beyond the moment, but I can't. It's as if my focus has turned to a pinpoint and all I can do is deal with the situation before me. I switch out the fuse, finish my shower, get dressed, go out to the patio...autopilot has taken control.

"Are we going to get another daddy?" Ben asks in his quiet way. He'd witnessed Bree's meltdown, but had kept out of the way until now.

He crawls on to my lap, his seven year old face still tanned from our trip to Mexico, his eyes wide with his innocent question.

I don't know how to answer. He's only seven; he'd followed his dad around like a shadow. Yeah. It's sinking in. Three weeks later, now that our house echoes with silence, reality is inescapable.

I hold him tight and bury my face in his hair. He smells so good. I think holding my kids is one of life's most amazing gifts. They're depending on me, I know. How could Sean leave us? He loved us, told us all of the time. How could he abandon us like this?

"I'd like another daddy someday," Ben whispers.

If only life were as simple as a child believes it to be.

"No one ever told me that grief felt so like fear."
-- C.S. Lewis, A Grief Observed

Chapter Seven

Routine. The word is like a mantra to me every morning when I take Bree to swim practice. Get up. Function. Most days I stay in the car while she's at the pool. Socializing is simply too much to handle. I wish I could describe how tired I am because it's unlike anything I've ever experienced. All I want to do is sleep, but when I do I see Sean in my dreams and don't want to wake up. Or I see his distorted face in a nightmare...glassy eyes, tongue sticking out sideways...and I hate that it's a memory.

I'm probably keeping us too busy, but it's hard to slow down. After swim team, the kids go to summer sports' camps. Again, I hang out in the car. Or I make calls. I never knew there'd be so many calls to make, so much business to take care of after a death. Credit cards. Social Security. Loans. Bank accounts. Run here. Run there. Fill out paperwork. Send in death certificates.

Widow. I still can't say the word without cringing. Amber and Sean...Sean and Amber...always said together for a decade. Now I call people and say, "Sean is dead. I'm his widow. We need to remove his name." I am erasing him, or at least that's how it feels. I hate it.

My couple friends don't understand why it's odd to be around them. I'm suddenly the third wheel. When I'm with them, all I feel is Sean's absence.

We travel a lot for Bree's swim team. On our last trip, I only packed shorts...no tops at all. We ended up buying t-shirts at the swim meet. It's like I'm in perpetual distraction mode even though I am trying my best to focus.

When we're not a sports' camp, we're home

remodeling. I'm painting, organizing, fixing things.
We go to movies.

Lasagna and other types of hot dishes appear at
my house every night thanks to friends in the
community. A cooler has been set outside our front
door. Every night at 5pm, food arrives. If we're not
home, it's a guarantee that the cooler will contain a
dish of some kind when we return.

People come and go, all with questions about
Sean, about our plans. I'm so sick of our story I can't
begin to tell you. I don't want to deal with it.

I'm seeing Victoria, a counselor specializing in
trauma and grief. She tells me that what I'm feeling is
normal, but it sure doesn't feel that way. The manic
feeling continues, the fear that if I stop moving, I'll
shatter.

I hate talking about my plans. Getting up in the
morning is a plan—that's about as far out as I can
think. Well, unless you're talking about travel plans.
I've scheduled several trips. Victoria says that's my
way of coping, of escaping the situation without
actually making any drastic changes like selling the
house. So we're going to Lake George, New York,
Sioux Falls, South Dakota, Puerto Vallarta, and
Washington, DC in our near future.

People raise their eyebrows at our traveling
spree, but I no longer care what the masses say. I'm
acting on instinct—right or wrong are things I don't
think about. I have an overwhelming need to prove to
the kids and myself that life is normal without Sean,
that we can still be happy, that I can make this work
as 'The Easton Three'.

The kids are going to a children's grief therapist.
I have Victoria and they have Sally. I thought it would
be best to split it up so I could say what I needed
without censoring myself...and vice versa. Say what
you will about therapy, but I'm a huge proponent of

seeking professional help when needed. They don't necessarily love their therapist, Sally, but it's necessary. Sometimes I feel like they're overly concerned with my feelings so I'm grateful they have someone to talk to like Sally. They're still sleeping me with me every night, unable to separate without worrying about my welfare.

My therapist, Victoria, advises me not to make any significant life decisions until a year has passed, says I'm not thinking clearly even if I believe I am. She said it would be best to wait three years before making a significant life change.

I don't know if I believe her. Right now I have money in the bank, feel trapped by current circumstance, feel restless for change. I'm satisfying the urge to flee by booking all of these trips. I don't know where we'd move to anyway. The city is tempting and familiar. I dream of the ocean, of Oregon or Washington, or somewhere warm like Florida. I thought about moving to South Dakota or Minnesota to be closer to my parents, but that feels like going backward.

Of course, maybe I don't have a choice. People have told me I won't be able to sell the house when I disclose the suicide.

I can't write either, not even an email. My journals are filled with disjointed ramblings and scribbled words, "grief sucks" over and over again, random drawings of tornadoes, and letters to Sean. As for anything professional, the words escape me. My focus is off.

Victoria tells me not to worry, says my creative energy is focused on day-to-day tasks, and assures me that it will come back someday. I'm scared she's wrong. What if my creativity and sense of security died when Sean did? What if a part of me died with him and I'll never have it back?

Fear is such a part of my life now. I hide it well, I admit. I smile, conscious of people being uncomfortable around me. I cry behind the locked door of my bathroom with the water running so the kids don't freak out. They've seen me cry, it's not like I'm afraid of them seeing healthy emotion; but they've also seen my temper explode at small things that used to never set me off. In the bathroom, I let the sobs come until I'm curled into a ball on the floor or huddled in the shower. I can protect them from that, if not much else. They're always looking to me at how to be and I don't want them to be as afraid as I am.

I'm terrified every day that I'm doing all of this wrong. Sometimes when I'm driving I experience flashes of seeing Sean hanging in my closet, hear snippets of our last conversation where I told him to go. I have to pull over to get a grip. I need to keep it together for the kids' sake.

Ben keeps asking if he's going to have another daddy someday, which I've been told is normal for a little boy who just lost his father. How do I explain to him that I'm not exactly in dating mode yet...can't imagine that I will ever be? I feel married, but this void in my life is huge. Amber and Sean for a decade, always said as one entity. A gaping hole has been ripped into my life, yet I can't imagine anyone but Sean being there.

I found a Young Widows Bulletin Board—an online support group—where women say to give up the idea of dating until the kids have left the house. That's eleven years from now. *Seriously?* Am I supposed to be alone for the rest of my life? Again the absence of Sean resonates in my heart. Maybe the other widows are wrong. Everyone's story is different.

Widow. Will I ever get used to that word?

The loneliness is suffocating. I reach out to every friend I've ever had, desperate for connection. I talk to an ex-boyfriend on the phone. He's divorced. He calls me in the middle of the night and fills the void for an hour or two. But it's all an illusion; none of it replaces Sean or our relationship. I need validation, which is also unlike me, but it's true that suicide feels like the ultimate rejection.

I think of the overheard words at the funeral, *"when your husband kills himself in your bedroom closet, it's like a giant fuck you to you."* I feel abandoned. The loneliness is like nothing I've ever experienced, as is the guilt for not being a good enough wife. So I travel, remodel, keep moving and talk to people I haven't spoken to years. I fling out in every direction in hopes of filling the gap left by Sean's death...but it's always there.

I love Victoria, she's been a lifesaver, assures me that I'm doing the right things, but I'm not sure she's right. Everything feels wrong, as if my skin no longer fits my skeleton. I'm so tired, unable to sleep, can't stop moving, can't focus. She says this is grief, this is the journey I can't avoid, tells me that she's walking with me, that I'm not alone.

I feel very alone.

* * * *

Someone tried breaking into my house—kicked at the frame of my bedroom window one night. I know it was the guy Sean fired before he died, Rodney. The silhouette of his body illuminated by the solar light looked like him—short and stocky. Sean had caught him stealing from the work site and had fired him on the spot. It hadn't gone well. Sean had come home with a bloody gash over his eye.

"Sean's dead," I scream as I leap from my bed, which is next to the window. "Leave us alone!"

The dogs are in the room, growling, teeth bared. The kids are crying.

I'm shaking from head to toe.

"Sean's dead," I scream again when the form kicks the window frame a second time. "Leave us alone! I'm calling the police, I know who you are."

The shadow leaves. I call the police but they take forever to arrive. When they do, they look at the disturbed dirt by the bushes and the cracked window frame as if it's nothing, ask me if I could have been dreaming.

No. I wasn't dreaming because I'm barely sleeping. I grab the machete we'd bought in Belize a few summers ago and put it next to my bed.

Days go by before Ben runs in from playing outside telling me that he saw Rodney parked at the end of the driveway watching him. We'd visited Sean's work sites many times and the kids could easily identify most of the men who'd worked for him. By the time I'm outside, I see the taillights of the truck moving slowly away.

Maybe he doesn't know Sean is dead and is looking for him, I don't know. Or maybe he wants to steal some tools. Either way, I don't call the police again. I change our phone number because we've been getting a lot of hang up calls. Perhaps that's Rodney, too. I confide this to my friends who look at me like I've lost my mind.

Victoria believes me, sees how afraid I am. She tells me to keep my cell phone with me at all times, and don't let the kids outside unless I'm with them.

This business of death is beyond exhausting. I cancelled his name on credit cards, but for some reason his name alone was on the mortgage after we refinanced last year. Dealing with the mortgage company has been nothing short of hell. Back and forth with death certificates and phone calls...so I stop. I'll deal with it later. I need a break.

Some days I shake so badly I can barely hold the phone to my ear. My hair is falling out in clumps.

My doctor says it's anxiety and suggests I start practicing yoga.

People don't know how to act around me, have admitted that I'm walking through their own nightmares so they don't know what to say. All of my friends are married...but I'm the widow now and I don't fit. I want to say, "Hey, I'm still the same Amber"...but that would be a lie.

I'm manic almost in my need to keep moving, to avoid sleeping. When I sleep, I see Sean's distorted face when he hung himself. I wake up in tangled limbs of kids sharing my bed and stare at the ceiling most nights. I'll sneak away from the kids to rearrange the family room in the middle of the night or start painting a hallway. It feels crazy, actually.

Victoria tells me it isn't crazy.

I'm beginning to question her credentials.

"The moon stays bright when it doesn't avoid the night."
-- Rumi

Chapter Eight

I have an overwhelming desire to organize everything in the shed. This has always been Sean's domain, but it's time for me to figure out what's in here and claim it as mine.

I open toolboxes...find empty liquor bottles. The first one makes me angry. Rum. I turn it over and over in my hands. I remember him looking me in the eye—even on that last day—and telling me that he wasn't drinking again. Lies, all lies.

As I continue to move things, more liquor bottles fall out from drill cases and from shelves. They're everywhere. Some empty, some not. I toss them aside, tears streaming down my face at the betrayal.

How many times had I come out here? He'd always been working on a project of some kind. He'd smile in that easy way he had, we'd talk, the kids would always be underfoot. Yet he'd been hiding his secrets the entire time.

More bottles stack up around my feet, tangible proof of his deception. I brace myself against the workshop, thankful that the children are playing outside. Tears fall unchecked. I feel as if I've been broken.

Lies, all lies. How many more betrayals would I discover? He'd sat there on the deck that day, his hand on my knee, looked me in the eye and asked me to trust him. Then he'd hung himself while we'd been making lunch. How could he do this to us, to me? I'd stood by him, damn it. I loved him...so much.

Anger flares like a wildfire in my blood. I toss the bottles into the trashcan, my body shaking from emotion.

What else will I find? I remember the sheriff questioning me about drugs. Was he on drugs? Did withdrawal from them cause his insane behavior during our vacation? Victoria asked me this once and I dismissed it. She said his behavior on the trip—even his paranoia—sounded like withdrawal.

Am I this naive? I used to come out here and sit on a log while he worked on some project or another. We'd talk. The kids would play. He had his stash within feet of me. I guess when we want to believe something with all of our heart, we become blind to what's in front of our eyes.

Maybe his suicide *is* truly my fault. I should have searched this earlier, trusted myself more. How many times had my intuition told me that he lied? But he'd accuse me of being paranoid, asked me what he'd need to do to win back my trust...all the while he'd been manipulating me.

I clean up the mess, wipe my tears, organize the tools, and process all of this information. My brain is at capacity. I'm not sure I can absorb much more.

* * * *

Victoria tells me that addicts are expert liars. I don't want to hear it. I'm tired of everything being excused by his alcoholism. I didn't deserve the lies and the kids sure as hell didn't. We were good people, loving and kind. How could he do this to us? All those years I'd thought he was sober...had it all been a lie?

Who was he?

"I'm so pissed off," I tell Victoria. "At the same time, I miss him. How can that be? What does that make me? Weak? Stupid? Codependent? And then I hate him for all the lies, for making me feel foolish for loving him. Does this make sense?"

"Addicts are two people. There's the addiction

part and then the man you loved. You can hate the addict and still love the man. It's okay."

"It doesn't feel okay." I shake my head, unable to stop the tears. "I feel like he had a mistress in our marriage, that the kids and I were never a priority. There was always this other thing that meant more to him and it won in the end. He chose the addiction rather than us. He didn't fight. He let us go rather than choosing sobriety. I hate that. And I feel horrible that I'm saying these things."

I feel horrible, sick to my stomach and nervous. I'm not used to this kind of anger raging through my bloodstream.

"I never wanted to be a single parent, to be judged. We were good people, all of us."

"Why does this change the fact that you're good people?" she asks.

"He lied. I lied for him. He killed himself in my closet. Whose lives are like that?"

"More than you know, Amber. Addiction doesn't discriminate. The best of people lose themselves." She takes out a tablet and draws a picture of two circles. One is much larger and overlapping the other. She points to the large circle. "This is the addict overshadowing the person. It's okay for you to be pissed as hell at the addict for his lies and bad decisions. That guy was an ass, a real bastard." She points to the smaller circle. "This is Sean, the man you miss, the guy who danced with you, who stargazed with you, who taught the kids to ski. It's okay for you to love this guy, to miss him."

"They're the same." I stare at the circles, understanding what she's saying but unable to reconcile it in my heart. Not yet. I'm so angry at this entire situation. "It's not fair."

"No, it isn't fair."

"He chose the addict."

"Perhaps he felt overwhelmed by it."

"Don't make excuses for him."

"I'm not. The addict lied to you, stashed liquor bottles, and pushed Sean over the edge. I'm not excusing him."

I think of the man at the funeral who came up to me at the end, hugged me, admitted he was from AA, and said not to blame Sean because he'd always talked about how much he loved us all. I can't stop crying. He didn't love us enough to stay.

"I never thought we'd end up like this." I think of handsome Sean, the guy who told me every day that he loved me, even when things were rocky between us. "I thought we'd make it. I thought love was enough, how stupid am I? I thought that if I loved him enough, he'd choose us. He never did. He chose alcohol and that's not fair."

I remember Pastor Vera's words from the funeral when she said that he had simply grown weary of the struggle. Was that the truth? Would I ever know? How do I forgive him? The kids miss him every day. I do, too.

"I'm sure he wanted to make it."

"He didn't try hard enough." I think back on our Mexico trip. He'd disappear for hours at a time. Had he been drinking there, too? Probably. He must have become skilled at hiding it...or I'd been blind.

"Addicts are expert liars. Don't blame yourself for not knowing," she says as if reading my mind. "It's okay for you to mourn Sean, the man you loved, the good guy you talk about, the kids' dad. It's okay."

"I always protected him, even at the funeral, even now. I'm an idiot." I can't believe I allowed myself to be manipulated like this. I'm an educated woman, had a great career once upon a time, and yet I fell for Sean's lies.

What was true? Was his love true? If so, then

how come he killed himself in our room? Maybe all of
it *was* a giant fuck you to me.

But how do I stop loving him? Is it possible?

"You're going to get through this, Amber."

"I'm not even sure what that means...get
through this. I'm not even sure who I am anymore
and I sure don't know what to do next. I'm winging it
every day."

"Winging it is a good thing." Victoria leans back
in her chair, smiles, and looks much more confident
in my sanity than I am. "Now you have a piece of the
puzzle you didn't have before, you can build from
here. You're going to be okay. I'm here. You're not
alone."

As I leave her office, I feel empty and
uncertain. I cried it all out, but now there's nothing
left.

"When you love someone, it's never over,' Dr. Carruthers replied gently. 'You move on, because you have to, but you bring him in your heart."
-- Elizabeth Chandler, Kissed by an Angel

Chapter Nine

To keep the soccer team together, I've taken over as head coach. Do I know anything about coaching a bunch of second graders? Nope, but here I go. I've purchased a book called "Soccer Coaching for Idiots," figured that summed it up nicely. I've received a few comments from the soccer moms about them being "surprised that I'm still living up here", "you're just Sean's wife, what do you know about soccer?" I've also been told, "you don't want to hear what they're saying on the sidelines." And you know what? No, I don't. The key word there is *sidelines*. These critics of mine have no idea what I'm thinking or feeling or dealing with day-to-day. I'm doing the best I can in a sad situation without much of a break to catch my breath. I'm not coaching the team for the parents...I'm doing this for the kids.

Sorting through Sean's soccer bag brought back a lot of memories. It's only been a few months. He coached his last game the day before we left for Mexico. His "Coach Sean" cap fell out when I opened the bag looking for orange cones to set up on the field.

Sometimes I feel like my face is going to split in two from the effort it takes to keep smiling when I want to hide.

I set the cap aside, laid out the cones, referred to the "Soccer for Idiots" book for some drills, and started practice. Seeing all of the kids laughing together and running around makes me happier than

I've been in months.

Routine. Keeping things the same. Again.

More often than not, I feel like the ultimate pretender. When Sean was alive, I covered for him, kept up the pretense of a happy marriage while we struggled to keep it together. I'm pretending that I'm fine now despite feeling like a zombie. I pretend that I don't hear the judgmental comments or that their words don't undermine my fragile confidence.

"Writing yet?" They ask.

"Here and there," I lie, not wanting to explain.

"You saying you're a writer is just fiction, isn't it? Writer is just another term for unemployed," a friend's father says after a soccer game.

It's been three months since Sean died. What do these people expect from me? I don't respond anymore. Let them think what they will. I have more important things requiring my focus.

I enjoy coaching soccer a lot more than I anticipated. It's fun watching a pack of seven and eight year olds running around the field. I stay on my side of the sidelines and ignore the parents. No, I'm not Sean, but, hey, we're having an undefeated season. Ben is laughing and happy that he's with the same bunch of kids he's played with since preschool. That means everything to me. I'm kind of goofy compared to Sean's coaching style, I'll admit that. I don't take it that seriously, but the kids are learning some awesome skills thanks to the books I'm reading. As far as I'm concerned, we have the best team in our league. *(Let me remind you of our undefeated status, please!)*

Ben went from advanced reading in first grade to being behind in second. His teacher is fresh out of college and doesn't understand the grief process so heaps on extra work for him every night. She sent home a note saying that I'm not doing enough to build his confidence and need to help him more at home. Ben's had fallouts with some friends who tell him that his daddy is burning in Hell—it's second grade so I can only assume that sentiment is coming from their parents

It's the same story with Bree, who went from doing very well to barely functioning in school. She's such a sweetie, so shy, and it's hard for me to see her struggling.

Off we go to Sally, the kids' grief therapist. Ben is only seven, almost eight, yet he'd been the first to find Sean hanging in the closet. Most adults go through their lives without witnessing such a horror. Why can't his teacher understand that he's recovering from trauma as well as grief? Why is that such a hard concept to understand? He misses his father, loves his daddy, and doesn't understand why anyone would tell him that Sean was bad and he can't talk about him anymore.

I get so angry at people's ignorance. I'm tired of taking the high road and being strong. I want to scream at people not to judge us, to leave the kids out of it, to defend Sean even while I'm angry at him.

All in all, the kick off to the school year is challenging, but we're doing the best we can.

Grief and trauma are two different things—combine them and they are a dastardly duo. Sally has gone above and beyond by taking time to visit the school to talk to the kids' teachers, but not much is changing.

I feel like I'm in constant fight mode as I'm standing up to the school system, coaching, dealing with the business of death, finding more liquor bottles hidden in obscure places, maintaining our routine, trying to keep life fun for the kids despite it all, defending Sean publicly even though I'm battling my own feelings, and deciding what to do with the house. *Fight, fight, fight.*

* * * *

Sean's mother wants to get together to celebrate his birthday. Is it okay to celebrate someone's birthday who has died? She never met with us when he was alive to do this, but now it seems like her highest priority.

Fine. Whatever. I'll try to suppress my urge to confront her about the "ultimate rejection" comment.

We meet in Denver for dinner and a movie. I'm not sure why she wanted to this because she's not speaking to the kids who are so desperate for a connection to their dad. She stares at me, eyes full of blame and hurt.

I don't know what to say. Sean would have been thirty-five today. All I can think about are should have beens and what ifs. It's an awkward night for everyone, another first on a long list of pending firsts coming our way. We're all missing the birthday boy, his absence an ache that I'm beginning to think will never dissipate.

"You cannot die of grief, though it feels as if you can. A heart does not actually break, though sometimes your chest aches as if it is breaking. Grief dims with time. It is the way of things. There comes a day when you smile again, and you feel like a traitor. How dare I feel happy. How dare I be glad in a world where my father is no more. And then you cry fresh tears, because you do not miss him as much as you once did, and giving up your grief is another kind of death."
-- Laurell K. Hamilton

Chapter Ten

Thanksgiving in Puerto Vallarta, Mexico is a welcome reprieve. It's my first time traveling out of the country with the kids as a solo parent. As we land, I feel the first quiver of trepidation.

All of the vacations I've taken since Sean's death were spent with friends or family with other adults as a buffer. Now it's sinking in...I'm a single mom traveling internationally with two kids. I needed Sean's death certificate to prove that I had the authority to take them out of the country.

We'd been a family of four during our last trip to Mexico. Was it really only five months ago?

Once at the resort, we rush to the ocean and play in the waves until sunset. I drink too much rum, but we're having fun. This is our first major holiday without Sean. I want to stay in motion, make sure the kids are happy. We swim with dolphins at a waterpark, walk the beach every night, play in the waves all day, and spend Thanksgiving Day riding horses to a waterfall.

Despite Victoria's reassurance, I feel like I'm avoiding reality by taking all of these trips. Running away. I'm trying so hard to make sure the kids are happy and to prove to myself that our lives haven't changed. That's ridiculous. I miss Sean so much I can barely stand it. Even here with the palm trees, sunshine, and ocean breeze, I miss him. I can travel the world and never forget, especially not here where we spent our honeymoon. What was I thinking?

Maybe that's exactly why we came here, my need to reconnect with a happier time. I take the kids to the restaurant he and I had found on our honeymoon. I tell them the story of how we'd found it by accident, had come here over and over again. I share all the happiness and the goofiness of that week with them. They love hearing stories of their dad. From the terrace of the restaurant, we watch an Aztec performance on the beach. A man in full traditional dress climbs up a pole at least four stories high while others dance in a circle on the beach. Once on top of the pole, he stands on a board about a foot wide and plays a flute. The kids are awestruck.

The Pacific stretches behind the scene, black except for the white of the waves caressing the beach where the performers are. Ben is in my lap, laughing. Bree is leaning over the railing of the restaurant, her face lit up with joy.

It's good to be here. I feel connected with a happy time—a time full of hope with my new husband. I feel like Sean's here with us, too.

Going home is bittersweet. This week away has been good for us. I slowed down and reconnected with a place I hadn't been since my honeymoon. As the plane takes off bound for the United States, we're all quiet. That's the thing with traveling...it always ends with returning to reality.

* * * *

I'm taking the kids up to Breckenridge to ski school every Saturday morning. Personally, I don't enjoy skiing, but it was Sean's thing. He had the kids skiing before they could walk so I feel it's important to keep this alive in them. So we travel to

Breckenridge every Saturday morning.

There are a lot of memories here for me—Sean and I dating, us skiing as a family, usually with him holding one of the kids on his shoulders when they were tots, and us lounging in the hot tub at the resort. He grew up here, would tell me stories about his youthful misadventures on the mountain. We'd go to Fatty's Pizza, made it a routine because he had a friend who was the bartender. I keep this routine alive, too, by taking the kids there every Saturday after I pick them up from ski school before we head out on the drive home.

What people don't understand is that Sean is more than his addiction and cannot be defined by his death. I'm trying to find peace with that, too. We had a life together, a lot of fun memories, and traditions of our own. I want the kids to know these things. They're so young that I'm scared they'll forget him, lose the identity he'd been bestowing upon them. I tell them everything I can remember of the stories he shared with me about growing up. I want his memory to live so I pass on what I know...and we go to ski school every Saturday morning.

I've had family members tell me they don't want me to ever mention Sean's name again because they hate him for what he did to us. I reject that idea. They can feel how they choose to feel, this is true. However, he was my husband, the father of my children, and I can also choose.

Am I angry? Yes. Sometimes I feel so angry I don't know what to do with that kind of energy. When bills are coming in, when people are badgering me about moving or not moving, when the kids are struggling, when I'm dealing with endless questions, when I wake up from a nightmare of seeing his handsome face distorted in death, you bet I get angry at him for leaving us.

That's the hard part to reconcile—the anger with the sadness.

But here on the mountain with the kids happy from skiing and us eating pizza at Fatty's, I'm choosing to be in the moment and perpetuate a tradition that Sean started. I want the kids to have a piece of their dad's life in the here and now.

Screw the critics.

"Grief can be a burden, but also an anchor. You get used to the weight, how it holds you in place."
--Sarah Dessen, The Truth About Forever

Chapter Eleven

Christmas. I've been dreading this for months. We're traveling to Washington, D.C. to be with my brother and my parents. I've sent all the Santa presents ahead of time. I'm pretty sure I'm overcompensating. Okay, yes. I admit it. I'm overcompensating with material things to distract the kids from the sadness of this first Christmas without their daddy. Is it the right thing to do? No, probably not. All I know is that I want them to be happy so I'm going above and beyond to make it so. I can't control what happened on May 29...but I can completely control Christmas morning.

A week ago, I finalized my will. The mortgage had finally been put solely into my name and I'd wrapped up all but one of the loose ends. The exhaustion has caught up to me. I'm on antibiotics and sleeping pills, neither of which seems to be doing much of anything.

I want this Christmas to be perfect, but feel my energy coming to an end. I'm hoping I'll be able to spend some time alone, maybe sleep, when I'm in D.C. It's fascinating to me how I have never thought about sleep so much in my life as I do now. I don't remember the last time I've slept more than a few hours at a time or without the kids wrapped around me. My nerves are shot.

Wrapping up the business end of Sean's death feels odd. My to-do list is gone. Now what? Go on with living, I guess, whatever that means.

But first...Christmas in D.C. I want it to be perfect so the kids don't miss their dad, but I know that's unrealistic. I'm only distracting them, but that's okay. For now.

I'm not what my family expected. I'm tired, out of it, distracted. My hands shake. My nerves are shot. I hear words like "time to snap out of it" and feel like a failure. Again. No one wants to talk about Sean except us three. It's as if he didn't exist. I'm accused of being selfish.

This isn't what I intended. Maybe my perception is off because I'm not sure what I'm doing that is so wrong. I let my guard down, am more exhausted than I can describe, and can't keep pretending that I'm okay.

I'm not okay.

I haven't spent one night alone since the moment we found Sean hanging in the closet. I've been in perpetual motion—my choice—and now I've hit the wall. Unfortunately, I've hit the wall here where people expect me to be in the holiday spirit. I'm letting them down. It feels as if all the energy I spent maintaining the to-do list has left all at once. I can barely stand. So tired.

Grief found me despite my accumulation of frequent flier miles. All this time spent running caught up to me. No matter how far I traveled or how busy I've kept myself, I couldn't outrun sorrow.

I am absolutely terrified that *this* is my new normal. What if I don't ever snap out of it? What does that even mean...*snap out of it*? Why is it bad to be sad? My husband died six months ago. Is it so horrible that I miss him? Is it wrong to be scared?

All I know is that I'm tired, that I'm unintentionally doing things that are pissing people off, that my nerves are shot, and that I hate feeling like this.

Correct that...I hate this entire situation.

* * * *

Being alone like this is more frightening than I ever anticipated. Grief isn't a 'condition' or an 'issue' to get over. It's the loneliest journey I've ever experienced.

Everyone leaves. Everyone who said "call me" doesn't answer the phone. This kind of alone is terrifying. It's different than being single, back when I had single friends who were available and plans were abundant. This is the absence of what was and what will never be. This is the realization my life plans have been thrown off course and I have no idea how to navigate this new path.

I feel almost desperate to connect with Sean. I wear his sweaters, look at photographs, watch our wedding video, wear his wedding ring on my thumb, and write him letters in my journal. I sit in my closet and talk to him out loud in the middle of the night. I ask him why he didn't choose us in the end. When I look at those pictures and videos, I stare at his face and wonder when he became so lost.

Bree has a stuffed monkey that she carries around. Sean bought it for her last Valentine's Day. When she presses the paw, a recording of Sean's voice says, "I love you, Breezy Bree." She's upset tonight because it stopped working. I thought it was a battery problem, but that didn't fix it. Another piece of him is gone.

"You can't do anything right!" She threw the monkey at me.

I'm holding it now as I sit in the closet where he died. Maybe I'm losing my mind. I tell him about my fears that I'm a horrible parent, my worry about letting everyone down, and tell him that I love him.

New Year's Eve is approaching. Normally, I look forward to the new year, but now all I see is a void of endless nights where I pace, scared to sleep for fear of seeing him in my dreams.

I ache, simply ache deep in my chest and I don't think it will ever go away.

He left us, damn it. He chose to go, yet here I am mourning him like a fool, pacing the house, wearing his sweaters, and holding a damn monkey while sitting on the floor where he died. There's not one thing that's right about this picture. Not one thing.

How do I get beyond this? What if I'm stuck here in this state of limbo, of not being able to think beyond the moment? How can I mesh the two parts of Sean? How do I make peace with any of this?

In DC, my family said they want the old Amber back, that they can't stand seeing me look so sad.

I don't think the old Amber exists anymore.

I feel like I'm in a soundproof booth, trapped behind glass. I see myself on the other side—a version of me that is happy, secure, and confident. I smack the glass with both hands in an attempt to break through to reach her, but the barrier won't yield. I'm trapped in this bubble of grief, nightmares, and regret.

"Grieving doesn't make you imperfect. It makes you human."
-- Sarah Dessen, The Truth About Forever

Chapter Twelve

Today is the first wedding anniversary without my groom. I buy carrot cake—Sean's favorite—and eat it alone in my bedroom after the kids have gone to sleep. Today would have been our tenth anniversary. We'd had plans to renew our vows in the Caribbean, a fresh start after a rocky beginning. It had given us something to work for, to believe in. I'd wanted more than anything for it to happen...but it didn't. Who knows? After what I've discovered in the past months, maybe it wouldn't have happened even if he'd lived.

Why did he make that vow renewal plan with me? Why did he spend our last night in Playa Del Carmen looking at wedding bands to replace his battered one if he knew he was going to die two days later? I've replayed our last conversation and our final vacation so many times in my mind looking for clues.

"Our wedding day was the happiest day of my life," he'd said as we walked along the beach. "You and the kids mean everything to me. I know I've made mistakes, but I'm going to fix everything. You deserve to be happy, Amber."

Without closing my eyes, I can visualize his feet walking in the sand next to mine and hear his voice as clear as if he were speaking now.

Had his plan for suicide already been cemented into his mind as he held my hand while we walked the beach? Now when I remember his words, they seem like goodbye.

I cry over carrot cake, my mind replaying everything from those last conversations to our honeymoon to the wedding itself. I have Sade's "King of Sorrow" playing on my iPod, not exactly pick-me-up music, but it suits my mood.

Every wedding anniversary he had duplicated my wedding bouquet and surprised me with it wherever we happened to be. How could such a romantic man leave his family? Lie to us? Questions remain. The man who knew the answers is gone.

It's such a struggle to mourn him when I'm angry with him for so many things. Peace is elusive.

The kids and I have already had so many firsts without Sean...first birthday, first Thanksgiving, first Christmas, now first wedding anniversary alone. There will be others in our future...high school graduations, weddings, grandchildren. Will I ever stop missing him? Will there ever be a day when I don't think about him?

I hug his pillow to my chest, not really caring about the abandoned cake, and cry for all those promises and plans that will never be.

* * * *

Last week, Bree came home with a dislocated shoulder and a black eye. A boy on the playground had bullied her.

Today she's in the grips of an anxiety attack while getting ready for school. Her body is as stiff as a board, breathing hitching on sobs, and face flushed red. She doesn't want to go back, but not because of the boy on the playground. Her teacher told her that if she couldn't read a book aloud in class that she couldn't go to lunch and would need to pay a dollar. I've had enough. What is wrong with these people? We've had Sally visit the teacher to discuss the grief/trauma combo and how that was adversely affecting Bree, but no one is listening.

Thanks to the other mothers on Bree's swim team, I have resources for home schooling. Did I ever think I'd be "one of those" people who homeschooled? No. Never. But this situation is out of control and isn't doing Bree any favors. I need to take matters into my own hands. I never thought I'd be a single mother, but this is how it is. I refuse to allow my daughter to experience anymore trauma, especially when this is a situation I can control.

"You're overreacting," my friend Aly says to me. "You're intolerant of other people's opinions."

"What opinions? My nine year old daughter is wearing a sling, has a black eye, and is scared to death of returning to school where no one seems to understand what she's been through."

"How long are you going to use Sean's suicide as an excuse?"

It's been six months. Where is this timetable that everyone is referring to? I've read a lot of books lately about grief and none of them contain a rulebook.

"The kids' grief therapist agrees with me about removing her from school. We all need time. By the way, it's not an excuse; it's a reality."

"You're being unkind to the teachers. They have a hard job and a lot of kids to manage. You can't expect them to give your child special attention," Aly says.

Fuck her. Fuck them all, actually.

I withdraw Bree from school, but leave Ben in the system. His teacher might be foolish with her criticism about his handwriting, but he loves school. And, to be honest, I have no idea what I'm doing so home schooling one child at a time is probably all I can handle.

"You're not thinking clearly," my cousin says.

"I think you've gone crazy. You're ruining her chances at a good education," another family member says.

I go Barnes and Noble and buy educational books. I stock up on supplies. I can do this. My intuition says I can. The moms from swim team say I can.

"You're being overprotective," another friend says.

I listen to their opinions, weigh the pros and cons, but the truth is that my gut is telling me that I need to take action. Protecting Bree from something within my control isn't being overprotective. If I've learned anything in the past seven months, it's that I can't shield my children from the world. I can, however, do something proactive about *this* situation.

I'm an educated woman. I can teach at a fourth grade level, for God's sake, it's not like I'm trying to teach her astrophysics.

"You're doing the right thing," Victoria says. "You need to listen to your intuition. So far every decision you've made has been what's right for you and the kids. That's all that matters right now. You're taking care of your family. I have faith in you, Amber. You have great instincts."

Victoria is my lifesaver.

We go to the Art Museum, call it a field trip. I enjoyed coaching and now I'm enjoying teaching. Am I writing? No. I'm thanking God for a large savings account that is slowly depleting. I'm budgeting as well as I can, dragging out the money so I can do what I need to do while I pray that my writing ability will return. I haven't written professionally since before our trip to Mexico.

Actually, I'd make a horrible employee at the moment. I fall asleep in odd places, rarely my bed. I can't think abstractly. My emotions are all over the place. My journal pages are stained with tears and scribbled repetitive sentences. Yeah, I'm thankful I have some breathing room so I can navigate this rocky road at my own speed.

Right now my focus is on my family and doing

whatever it takes to get us all through this as best as I can. Only time will judge if I'm making good decisions. Both Bree and I understand that home schooling is a temporary option. We're slowing down our pace, concentrating on one thing at a time. I like having her around, having lessons planned throughout the day, structured time, and juggling the kids' activities in the evenings.

To schedule some time alone, I've started having monthly massages, usually after a therapy session with Victoria. Bree waits outside with her books, content with the arrangement. During the massage, I can feel the stress leaving my body with every stroke on my muscles. I've been storing all the emotion in my body, unable to find an appropriate release. Massage helps me feel like I'm taking care of myself, it's my oasis in the midst of chaos.

I bought a fishing license. My first. Ben and Sean used to fish so...that's what we're going to do. I'm even wielding a chainsaw to cut down dead trees. I know I can't replace Sean, nor do I wish to become a manly woman, but I'm starting to believe that maybe...just maybe...we're going to be okay.

"Grief is like a moving river, so that's what I mean by it's always changing. It's a strange thing to say because I'm at heart an optimistic person, but I would say in some ways it just gets worse. It's just that the more time that passes, the more you miss someone."—Michelle Williams

Chapter Thirteen

I take my wedding rings on and off, sometimes throwing them against the wall or hiding them in the jewelry box. On and off they go depending on my mood. Today they're on and I'm twisting them around my finger.

I am not married anymore. The reality of that weighs me down like cement blocks tied to my ankles. Widow. I'm not sure I'll ever get used to saying that word.

I know that elderly widows and widowers wear their rings indefinitely; but I'm young. At least that's what people keep telling me...*"you're young, you can get remarried again, Sean died not you."*

The idea of dating or remarrying or anything remotely like that can't penetrate the fog in my brain. My heart aches for my husband, yet the reality is he's never coming home. So what am I? Technically, a widow. Emotionally, a wife.

Today I'm thirty-eight. Birthdays always make me think of the future and what –ifs. Today isn't any different.

I laugh a little at the idea that thirty-eight is young when just a year ago I thought thirty-seven was old. It's strange how one's perspective can change in such little time.

I twist the rings on my finger, debating on whether it's right or wrong to wear them. I understand that they're only rings, a material symbol that won't change how I feel in my heart; yet the idea of removing them permanently is too much to contemplate.

The young widows bulletin board goes back and forth on this subject. I'm not the only one who struggles with the issue. The consensus is that I'll know when it's right to take them off permanently. Today I'm wearing them because the weight of them on my finger makes me feel secure and reminds me of a man who loved me.

* * * *

With the one-year anniversary of Sean's death approaching, I'm getting nervous about what to do. Do I mention it to the kids? Do I let it slide by as if it's nothing even though it was the single most important day of my life so far? Although I keep telling everyone who'll listen that I refuse to allow Sean's suicide to define my life, it has. What do I do with this day, especially when so many people around me don't like me mentioning his name?

Memories of all that happened a year ago return like flashes of lightning...a family of four going to the kids' spring concert at school, Sean disappearing for days with no explanation, unexplained cash withdrawals, him telling me that he wasn't drinking again and wondering if I'd ever trust him, us going on a ten day family vacation to Mexico to 'reconnect'. All of it, the good and the bad, haunt me at unexpected moments.

I know Sean was a flawed individual, but he was *my* flawed man. I wasn't the best wife either, I know. We were young, just like everyone is—usually—when they get married. Although I agreed to stay home with the kids and give up my career, I admit now that I resented the dependency even though I loved spending time with my children. Because of that, I probably started more than my share of arguments and overscheduled volunteer commitments.

I know his alcoholism played a part in my resentment—all those late nights of scrambling to get the kids bundled into the car, leaving him, pretending all was well to the outside world. Why didn't I divorce him years ago? Because I loved him—not in an enabling way because he knew I didn't support his addiction. Our multiple separations were proof of my intolerance. No, I loved him with my entire being and wanted him well. I'd look at him and see the good guy there worth fighting for. He fought, too. But our marriage was a roller coaster ride with intense highs and lows—him getting sober, us staying together, being happy, believing he was on solid ground, then having it ripped out from beneath us. Despite all of that, I never anticipated suicide would be our ending.

He gave up the fight, yet here I am still protecting him and battling to hold the pieces together. I resent that...and feel guilty for it.

How do I reconcile all of this? Guilt. Resentment. Sorrow. Anger. Frustration. Fear. Yet there's a lot of laughter with the kids...and sometimes I feel guilty for that, too. Here I am raising two kids who need me to be the best version of myself—we laugh, we travel, we make new memories—yet a part of me feels simultaneously guilty and pissed off that he gave up. It's exhausting, more tiring than I know how to explain, to combat all of these emotions on any given day while putting one foot in front of the other because life doesn't stop moving forward.

People are putting the pressure on me to get a job outside the home despite my need to home school Bree. It's as if they think I'm making up her anxiety.

"You need to get out with people," they say.

I'm with people every day between volunteering at Ben's school, taking the kids to their lacrosse and swim practices, and various other activities.

"How can you live in that house where Sean died? It's creepy. Everything in your life is the same, how can that be healthy?" they ask.

Victoria, Sally, and every book I can find says not to make any other major life decisions for one to three years after his death. Why do I need to explain this to anyone? They're not living my life.

"Don't you care about money?! You need to get a full time job again before you're too old and your savings is gone."

Gee, thanks, for the added pressure. Yes, I care about money, who doesn't? I can't write, am in a constant fog. I'd probably get fired from being one of those people holding signs on the side of a road right now because I'm not myself. But, thanks for telling me I'm getting old on top of that.

"You need to start dating, snap out of it, get on with your life."

Yeah, dating sounds like a lot of fun when I have one child with severe separation anxiety, still cry every day for my late husband, and can't form an articulate sentence beyond the elementary school level. If dating is anything like it was in my 20's, I can confidently say I don't have the energy for that right now—maybe ever.

Stop! No more unsolicited advice from those who mean well but cannot relate to my situation.

As the death day anniversary approaches, I'm haunted by it all. It's as if the memories break through cracks in my mind one at at a time. Random. Vivid. I'm being forced to remember it all, whether I want to or not. The comments from those on the sidelines aren't helping. All I want is an escape.

I schedule a trip to the Dominican Republic over the death day anniversary. Yes, the bank account is inching downward and people are rolling their eyes over my travels, but this vacation feels like salvation.

Victoria agrees, once again saying I'm making

good decisions. I wonder if her degrees are genuine.

In addition to the young widows support group, I've also joined Survivors of Suicide. Both are helpful. I need to be with people who 'get it', even if only in an online setting. I vent my most troubling thoughts in these online forums and am surprised when others have had the same experiences. It's not 'just me', after all.

In Survivors of Suicide, I hear others talk about the judgment they've experienced from people outside the realm of understanding. I don't wish my circumstance on anyone else because it's been a nightmare; but I'm truly grateful to find others who know what it's like to love someone despite their final act in this lifetime. This group understands...and they encourage me to remember as I see fit.

The Young Widows Bulletin Board helps me get through the lonely nights, works through parenting questions, and widow dilemmas. When I posted about possibly taking the kids to the Dominican Republic over the first year death day anniversary, they unanimously supported my decision.

My friends here are at a loss as to what I'm doing and why. They don't have any frame of reference for what I'm experiencing. Perhaps I expected too much of them, which is unfair. After all, some of them are younger than me and I'm only thirty-eight.

A good friend, someone who I thought of as a sister, told me she didn't have the energy to deal with my situation. She's not the only one. This past year has been loss after loss, usually from people I'd never expected to walk away.

It's happened with the kids, too. A year ago, they were inundated with play dates and birthday party invitations. That's all ended. Maybe people think tragedy is contagious? I'm not sure, but I do know the loneliness is amplified.

I've accumulated a team over the past several months: Victoria, Sally, Pastor Vera, Deanne (a Stephens Minister from the church who works with people in crisis), Survivors of Suicide, and Young Widows Bulletin Board. I'm learning that I'm no longer the same Amber who lived a year ago, will never be that woman again. My team is helping me be okay with that.

I feel like I need to hide. I'm sad and people don't like that. I try my hardest to put on a smile, to be as cheerful as I can around others, but there's an underlying sadness I can't shake. When I do let my guard down, it's usually met with criticism. I'm shutting people out, putting up a shield.

I found a note from Sean today tucked inside my favorite book of poems by Rumi. It's like being haunted after all this time. It said simply: *Never forget how much I love you—Sean.*

He'd always been one to leave me love notes. Seeing one now, though, brings everything crashing back. If he loved me so much, why did he leave? I'm mad. I've lost everything—my husband, my friends, my trust, my security.

I have a right to be sad. I'm tired of people telling me to shrug it off and move on as if I simply had a bad day. Life as I had known it to be ended when Sean died—same goes for the kids who are still processing the fact that he's never coming home.

So many questions come up with this note. When did he write it? Did he plant it there before he died knowing I'd find it after he'd gone?

"No, Sean, I don't know how much you loved me. It doesn't feel like love to me when you left me here all alone to deal with everything."

I burn the note in the wood stove. I stare at the edges curling with orange flames. It's all so pointless, it seems. What did our marriage mean? What was the point of all those battles to get him sober? How can he say he loved me when he left me alone? I never gave up on him, not even in the end. He gave up. I close the door to the woodstove, walk to my room, toss my wedding bands onto the dresser, and curl myself around a pillow. That's when the sobs come. I can't hold them back anymore.

I've lost so much in such a short time. I'm letting everyone down, even myself. I'm constantly telling Victoria that I won't let his suicide define me, but you know what? It already has. I feel like a giant 'S' has been branded into my forehead for all to see.

I'm so lonely that it's an ache that rips me to shreds. There's a difference between being alone and being lonely. I used to like being alone—would crave solitude—but this feeling is gut wrenching.

I don't know who I am anymore. Now I'm a widow, a single mom, and a woman whose husband committed suicide. I feel as if I am scarred. Damaged. How do I move on from this when I haven't really dealt with it yet? Sure, I checked off the to-do list, have gone to therapy, but I'm realizing now that I haven't even begun to face the sadness. Going to that dark place would mean letting go of control. I'm not sure I want to do that. What if I never come back? What if I get lost in despair?

Back in college I had a boyfriend who told me—during a rather heated phone call after a break up gone bad—that I'd end up alone. His words from over a decade ago whisper in my mind now despite Sean's love note from beyond the grave.

What if I do end up all alone? What if this is my fault and I just can't see it? No, Sean, I don't know how much you loved me!

The pain clenching my stomach as I sob is worse than any stomach flu I have ever experienced.

It's deep, unyielding, heart breaking.

"I thought, possibly, that what I really needed was to go where nobody knew me and start over again, with none of my previous decisions, conversations, or expectations coming with me."
-- Maggie Stiefvater, Forever

Chapter Fourteen
The Dominican Republic/May 2006

As I look down on the Caribbean Sea, I'm struck with panic. What am I doing taking two young kids to a country I've never been before? I know nothing about the Dominican Republic. I chose it because it's new, a place I'd never been with Sean, and because the pictures were breathtaking. How is that for great decision-making skills?

As we land, I see thatched roof buildings of the Punta Cana airport. Thump, thump goes my heart. Bree clutches her well-traveled bunny to her chest. Ben fires off a thousand questions about the island, the thrill of adventure shining in his eyes.

Humidity assaults us like a wet blanket when we exit the plane. The kids are excited when they hear steel drums playing and see women dressed in multi-colored sarongs balancing baskets of bananas on their heads. They pose with us as soon as we enter the airport and our picture is taken. Either they really know how to welcome tourists here or they're making sure we're not international terrorists by running us through a facial recognition program. Okay, so maybe I've seen too many spy shows. It's fun and festive already—a wonderful welcome.

My Spanish isn't working here. It's more of a combination of Italian and Spanish that the people are speaking. I go with it, do the best I can. After Customs, it's mayhem. In one corner of the open-air lobby is yet another group playing steel drums while taxi drivers line the exit shouting for attention. In front of us are the tour operators holding signs. I see our driver—or at least I think he's our driver. He points to an old school bus in the parking lot and has someone picking up our luggage.

The kids look worried with the disorganization. To be honest, I'm getting a bad feeling. Of course, I haven't slept in about 2 days now so that probably has something to do with my unease. No one else joins us on the school bus. Yeah, now I'm getting worried. I'd like to go out and ask someone else if we're in the right place, but I don't want to leave the kids alone.

A weird guy who possesses only two teeth in his mouth from what I can see walks onto the bus and asks me where my husband is. I hesitate before telling him that it's just us three. The kids are looking at me, eyes wide waiting for me to answer.

"Is this the bus going to Barceló Palace?" I ask instead.

He laughs, says something in Spanish I don't understand, and leaves.

"Let's get off," I say to the kids. "This isn't right."

"But our bags are already in the back," Bree says.

"We'll get them. Let's just get off and figure this out. We're not the only tourists going to a big resort, something's not right." I grab them and exit.

Man, it's hot. All I want at this point is to get to the hotel and find a pool. Exhaustion is allowing self-doubt to rear its head.

I find the man with our tour company sign and attempt to explain our situation. I'm realizing that my years of Spanish that work fine in the United States and Mexico are useless here. Or maybe I'm just rusty. Or tired. I hear more Italian than Spanish, or at least that's what it seems to me. Sure enough, he'd sent us to the wrong bus. We were supposed to be on a van!

He tells the creepy two-tooth guy to get our luggage while he leads us to the correct mode of transportation. Yes! Other tourists who look as confused as I feel.

So much for the festive feeling of only a few minutes ago. They should have met the plane with rum instead of steel drums. I need a drink.

Creepy two-tooth guy crawls into the van, puts his arm around me, and says something that makes the van driver laugh. I'm not amused. Ben crawls onto my lap.

I give creepy two-tooth guy my best bitchy American look that finally shuts him up and he leaves. An older American couple behind me asks if we're okay. I say yes and relax back into my seat. Bree is staring out the window making sure our luggage makes it to the van. It does.

As we look out the windows on our way to the resort, it's obvious how foreign this place is. A cow head hangs above a store entrance in town—someone says that's how the storeowners display that they have fresh meat. We pass acres of sugar cane with workers using machetes to clear paths.

Pat Benatar is playing on the radio, the driver is singing along in broken English. Eighties rock-n-roll in a van full of confused tourists traveling down the highway at break neck speeds while we pass cow heads hanging from stores.

What the hell have I done? Where are we?

I start laughing at the absurdity of it all. The kids start laughing, too. Pretty soon the entire van is laughing and I'm pretty sure we're all thinking the same thing. God, I love traveling. I do. It's fun how complete strangers can bond over the oddest situations.

Mayhem greets us at the resort. Spaniards are crowded around, all yelling and looking upset. Their tense energy is in direct contrast to the serene setting around us. Tall ceilings draped with vines and flowers, a waterfall along one wall, birds chirping, palm trees swaying...yet a bunch of Spaniards yelling at the center of it all.

The concept of a line seems to be as foreign as the country I'm in. We've been traveling for twelve hours—took the overnight flight from Denver to Atlanta to catch the connecting flight to the D.R.— and we're tired. I tell the kids to sit on our luggage and not move or talk to anyone while I join the fray to check in at the front desk.

I may not be Spanish—and I may be a woman born and raised in the Midwest US who was taught manners—but, damn it, I want my room and I want it now. I press in with the Spaniards, looking over my shoulder every thirty seconds or so to make sure my blonde haired babies haven't been stolen. They sit there, looking at me with tired but happy faces through the crowd. Bree clutches her bunny, gaze glued to mine. Ben is sitting on top of my flowered suitcase, feet swinging in the air, smiling at the madness.

Someone tells me that a bus of Spaniards arrived after their reservations at another resort had been mixed up, hence the mass confusion. A resort employee hands me a mojito in apology. I gladly accept.

Eventually, I have the keys and an escort to our room. Beautiful is an understatement. Our room is right on the beach, a junior suite (all the rooms here are) with a foyer and French doors opening onto a white sand paradise. No chaos here. Bliss.

Flowers of every color imaginable line our terrace. Palm trees sway in the breeze. Caribbean waves lick the beach only feet from where we're standing. A warm breeze slides across my skin, reminding me I haven't showered or changed clothes since yesterday. I feel the tension leave my body.

The maids are still cleaning our room so we sit outside drinking Cokes and marveling at the view in front of us. It's better than any picture could have captured. A catamaran zips across the sea, just off shore. The smell of hamburgers drifts through the air, reminding me of how hungry I am. Somewhere someone is playing steel drums...again. It's magnificent.

As soon as we can, we're in our swimsuits and on the beach. People back home may judge me as reckless or impulsive, but I needed this more than I can say. So did the kids who are riding their swim noodles in the waves and laughing. I have my rum punch in hand as I wade in the ocean with the kids at my side and face the horizon.

It's been a helluva year. All of that tension rushes out of me. I feel this incredible release as I float next to the kids, careful to prop my rum punch on my knee, feel the support of the salt water beneath me, and look up at the flawless blue sky.

A year ago today we'd been in Mexico, a family of four...I shake the idea from my mind. I can't believe it's been a year. I feel like I've been in perpetual motion for the past twelve months.

"Hamburgers!" Ben yells before dunking me in the water, effectively spilling my rum into the Caribbean.

We'd just seen the sequel to 'Pirates of the Caribbean' before coming down here. He's wielding his swim noodle like a sword, quoting Captain Jack Sparrow, and chasing Bree from the waves onto the white sand.

I guess we're having lunch. We wrap ourselves in cover-ups, grab our flip-flops, abandon our noodles, and towels on our chosen lounge chairs before following the scent toward a bar and grill on the beach. This is an all-inclusive resort, but not the buffet kind. There are restaurants tucked throughout, complete with menus.

There aren't many people here, I realize. After the scene in the lobby, I'd expected crowds everywhere, but that's not the case. It's actually very peaceful. Quiet.

After ordering hamburgers for all of us, I look around at the brightly colored buildings of the resort. A lake like swimming pool is nestled between them all, a swim up bar with a thatched roof is adjacent to where we're sitting. I figure out that's the source of the perpetual Caribbean music drifting across the sand.

A man is across from me, his long frame settled into the chair while his black hair falls across sunglass covered eyes. Teenagers are around him, talking amongst themselves as he stares out to sea. I can't help but notice him. He's got that aura about him that only some people possess without trying—that certain something that makes them stand out in a crowd.

I'm lonely. I miss having an adult partner. I realize that as I watch the man stare out to sea despite his crowded table, hear Ben quoting Captain Jack in his version of a pirate voice, see couples walking hand in hand along the beach, and remember why it is we're here now, just us three.

I'm happy, thankful that we have the means to escape reality for a bit. I'm realizing, though, that no matter how far I travel or how beautiful my surroundings, I can't escape being a widow.

Looking at that man, I wonder if that's how I look. Lonely. He seems alone even though a table of people surrounds him. I wonder if my inside feelings somehow transmit themselves to observers when I let my guard down. I hope not. I've tried so hard not to let the wounds be visible.

I turn my chair so I don't see him, focus on Ben's pirate talk, enjoy a great burger on beautiful beach in a place we've never been, listen to the sound of the waves accompanying the voices around me and the subtle music in the air, and soak up the reality of where I am in this moment.

* * * *

After a much needed nap for all of us, I call my parents and let them know we're alive. I call my cousin, chat about the flight. There it is again...this need for adult interaction.

We'd arrived before noon Punta Cana time so, even after a romp in the water, lunch, and a nap, it's only late afternoon. The kids are going back and forth between swimming pool and ocean, not making up their minds on where to settle in. They're happy, though, so it's okay.

So am I despite this sudden ache for an adult companion. The sea always calms me, makes me happier than any other place on earth. Perhaps that's why we've traveled so much this past year...my need for the sea.

Perhaps it's the rhythm of it, the sound that blocks out everything else, the ease of the Caribbean lifestyle. I watch the kids making a sand tunnel slash castle on the beach and realize that I am happy here. This is good. New memories.

"You are American?" A man with an accent I don't recognize asks. He's older than me by at least ten years, definitely South American from the looks of his black hair and even darker eyes. He sits next to me on the beach and points to a younger version of himself playing in the waves. "That is my son."

I realize this is the man from the burger restaurant.

"I'm American, yes. Colorado."

"I'm from Sao Paulo, Brazil." He smiles and I relax. Rum punch has a way with me...a good way. "We are here for six weeks, performing."

"You perform?" Sun, rum, and heat...a brilliant combination.

"I play saxophone in the band. Are you coming to the performance tonight?"

"We just got here a few hours ago...I don't know."

"You should come. How long are you staying?"

"Ten days."

"Only ten days?" His smile catches me off guard, a flash of white against dark skin. "You Americans never stay anywhere long, do you?"

I'd thought ten days was a long time when making the reservation. I laugh at the idea. "Do you travel a lot? Perform at resorts?"

He nods, stretches out on the lounge chair next to me. "We were in Cuba before here."

His son comes up to him and says something in a language I can't recognize. Portuguese, I realize. If I can't understand the Spanish their speaking here, there's no way in hell I'm going to figure out Portuguese.

"Come to the show. I will see you later." He stands abruptly, yells toward his son, and leaves. Just like that.

Interesting. Brazilian saxophone player. Yeah, that's probably not a good thing. Back in the day—pre-Sean—musicians were my downfall. Throw in a sexy accent, black hair, and that's all too much to handle. Brazil, huh? I've never met anyone from Brazil before...not that we'd met, per se, because our conversation lasted a minute, but...interesting.

I look back at the kids who are now slapping each other with their swim noodles and not in a

playful way. Time to shower, change, and explore the
resort a bit. Our overnight flight was catching up to
us all. I had no idea if it was the rum, or finally
relaxing, or sleep deprivation, but...had he been
flirting with me? No. Can't be. Then again...maybe.

I'm not sure I know how to react to that idea.

* * * *

We meet with the concierge in the lobby to plan
some excursions for our stay. It's much calmer now
so we absorb the beauty of it—marble floors, flowers,
towering ceilings, open walls, fountains. A golf cart
train goes by and we're told that it visits all the hotels
within this resort complex. Of course Ben wants to
go immediately, but I convince him to wait. We
arrange our tours, all of which seem very exciting to
me, too. I'm happy that I came to a place that's just
ours, no memories of Sean here. No one knows us. In
fact, from looking around the resort, it seems like
we're three of only a handful of blonde haired blue-
eyed people in sight.

I like that it's completely different from
anywhere we'd been before—all of our travels during
the past year were familiar, places where I'd share
memories of Sean. But the Dominican Republic is
now ours alone. That means something to me.

The other blondes are from France. The kids
have made friends with their kids and are now playing
'monkey in the middle' with them. There are also
some children from Santo Domingo, D.R. here that
are joining in on the fun. The pool feels like a friendly
United Nations meeting where the parents are kept
happy at the swim up bar while their kids—none
speaking the same language—play ball in the water.

I'm floating on my blow up raft when the
Brazilian shows up again. He pretends like he's going
to tip me over, swims beneath me, and shakes the raft
from below. When he surfaces, he says something I

don't understand—I'm not too sharp with accents.
Eventually, I understand. We talk about all the places
he travels, the fact he is with a large group of people,
that he speaks seven languages. We hang out in the
hot tub, laugh over drinks in the sunshine with our
kids always in sight. It feels good. Easy. Natural.

He never asks if I'm divorced or widowed—
nothing—and I like that. I've spent a year talking
about Sean or dealing with Sean-related matters. I
don't want to bring him up to the Brazilian. Not now.
I like that he's a professional saxophone player. I like
it even more that I can barely understand him at
times.

We drink mojitos, him attempting to explain
the secret to making a good drink in his thick
Brazilian accent, while we sit at the swim up bar
which is an island in the middle of the lake-like pool.

Bree and Ben have collected a pack of buddies
who are all floating around the pool on swim noodles,
all speaking a different language, and laughing in the
sunshine.

Life is good. Here. Now. There's something
incredibly freeing about being with strangers.

* * * *

Our first excursion on the island involves a
river tour in a duck boat beneath the Stone City.
From there we venture off to La Romana where we
board a speedboat with about a dozen others bound
for a private island. Bree is a natural in the water.
While snorkeling, she surprises me by free diving to
the bottom to pick up shells. This reminds me of
Sean—the adventurer who knew no fear, the guy who
propelled me off a boat in Belize to swim with sharks,
the man who taught his daughter to boogie board a
year ago.

So much for not thinking of him. He's here in
the eyes of my children, in their laugh, in their innate

athletic ability (that definitely didn't come from me). I came to a new place to make memories of us as we are now, not rehash the old. Anger surprises me in its sudden flash through my system.

I find the rum punch and settle in the shade. There's a makeshift dance floor in the middle of the sand. Off to the side is a hut where our lunch will be served in a few minutes. I take a minute to dry off and push the thoughts away. I want to listen to the salsa music, chat with the other tourists, snorkel with my kids, and play on this island.

Ben hangs with me in the shade while Bree runs back and forth in the waves. When I relax, unwanted memories pierce my consciousness. I try to focus on the people taking salsa lessons while wearing sarongs and swimsuits.

I miss Sean. I can travel far and often, but I miss him. That's the problem. I miss someone people don't like discussing. I miss someone I try not to remember because of the pain it causes. I miss being a wife. I miss having a plus one.

"I'm having so much fun," Bree says as she settles into the shade with us, her barbecue sandwich propped on her knees. "This is so cool. Do you think they filmed 'Pirates of the Caribbean' here?"

Cue Ben and his pirate voice.

These two are obsessed with Captain Jack.

* * * *

Once back at the resort, we take the golf cart train throughout the property, getting off here and there to check out the other hotels in the complex. We end up eating at a restaurant where every time someone orders a steak, the waiters run around waving white napkins while the sound of "moo" comes from speakers. It's not exactly classy, but it's funny as hell. We laugh every time. It's great, all this laughing.

We walk home to our place via the beach. The kids spot meteors but I miss them every time. What a beautiful island. Security guards are everywhere so I don't feel at all intimidated. Perhaps that's because of the rum...or the sun...or simply being a thousand miles from home.

We hang out on the beach for a few hours, looking at the sky and listening to waves. I love the ocean so much, yet live on top of a mountain. Go figure.

As we continue walking the beach, we see a film crew making a movie. There are lights, cameras, crew, makeup, actors we don't recognize. We watch for a while, eventually discovering that it's all in Spanish. I guess that explains why even the crewmembers are gorgeous.

At the edge of the resort, I see the Brazilian sitting alone in one of the restaurants. He's staring out to the blackness of the sea, hair blowing back from his face, posture one of contentment and confidence. I wish I understood him better. For all I know, he's been telling me his life story yet I'm clueless as to what that is. We walk past him. I know he sees me, but I don't acknowledge him.

After the kids are asleep, I go onto the terrace alone. I love watching the sea at night with all of its vastness. We missed the show, the one where the Brazilian plays his saxophone. I'd heard it from here earlier, though, and thought about going but the kids were worn out from their day.

It'd been a good day, complete with mooing and goofiness.

"Are you ever coming to the show?" The Brazilian asks from the sidewalk beyond the flowers bordering the terrace. He's so dark, dressed in black with his ebony hair.

"Eventually." I'm startled. I can hear the

television from my room and am conscious of the
kids sleeping. I wonder how he knows where my
room is, but then remember pointing it out to him
the other day when we were drinking mojitos at the
swim up bar.

"Can I sit with you? Talk?"

"I'll come over there. Wait." Again, I'm aware
of the kids in the room, not sure what I'm doing or
why.

That's not true. I like talking to him. More than
that, I like that he has no idea what happened to me a
year ago and no interest in finding out. To him, I'm
simply an American woman on vacation with zero
worries. I want to be that woman.

I meet him on the sidewalk and we sit on the
sand. I don't know where the perpetual salsa music
comes from, I've decided. I'd thought it came from
the swim up bar, but here it is late, after midnight,
and I can still hear it on the beach. Soft music, not
obnoxious.

"Do you salsa?" he asks.

"No, I don't."

"I will teach you."

And he does. There on the beach in the
moonlight with the quiet music, we dance. I'm
wearing my pajama pants, I realize far too late. So
much for glamorous. My hair is in a ponytail, I'm
wearing black pajamas, and no make-up. He teaches
me to salsa on the sand, never once complaining
when my bare feet step on his, his soft accented voice
guiding me.

Then he kisses me.

It's been over ten years since anyone but Sean
has kissed me.

It's intense, passionate, unexpected.

I apologize and go inside. He follows and
knocks at the door. I lock it, turn off the lights, curl

into bed next to Ben, and cry.

I cry because I liked being kissed by the Brazilian and dancing in the sand. I'm not sure I should.

* * * *

"Mom, there's your friend," Ben says when we walk into the main restaurant of the resort for breakfast.

Yep, there's the Brazilian. He's with his entourage of loud South Americans. From the looks of things, they'd all been up doing something athletic already. Don't these people sleep? Or maybe they hadn't gone to bed yet, I'm not sure.

We ignore them and find what has become our "usual" table in the corner. We've labeled it ours because it has only three chairs. Bree claims it was made specifically for a family of three. I'm inclined to agree.

The Brazilian and his group leave. On the sidewalk, he walks past us toward the beach with his son, leans over the bushes separating our table from the sidewalk, and smiles.

"What are your plans for the day?" he asks all of us, making a point to look at the kids.

"We're going shopping!" Bree's thrilled with today's plans.

"Tomorrow we're going to a cave and to see where Columbus was," Ben pipes in, already anticipating tomorrow's excursion to Santo Domingo.

"Are you coming to the show tonight?" He turns his attention to me.

I know he probably finds a woman at every venue to flirt with...or at least I tell myself that. He doesn't have the 'player' vibe to him, seems simply like a nice guy who happens to be lonely, too. Then again, what do I care?

* * * *

We go to the show. Finally. It only took us
three nights to get here. Ben likes pointing out the
Brazilian who nods in our direction from stage. I'm
reminded why I used to have a thing for musicians
back in the day.

It's much later that night, after the kids are
asleep, that I meet him on the sidewalk again. We talk.
We dance. We laugh. We kiss...the world doesn't end.
I'm not struck by lightning. Guilt doesn't torment me.
In fact, I feel like I'm waking up from a long sleep.

* * * *

Death day. We're in Santo Domingo visiting an
aquarium, Columbus's brother's house, the capital,
shopping in downtown, and exploring a cave. It's an
all day adventure that ends with a tour of tobacco
factory where we see a demonstration on rolling
cigars. Busy, busy, busy.

The shaking has returned to my hands and I
know it's because I can't help but remember every
detail of what we were doing a year ago compared to
what we're doing today. I hate that I can't suppress
the images no matter how hard I try. We're having
fun, soaking up a different culture, and laughing more
than we've done in twelve months.

The kids want to go back to the moo restaurant
(that's what we call it anyway). As soon as we get back
from the trip to Santo Domingo, we get in the golf
cart train and head out for some steak. I love this
place. The Barceló resort has several different hotels
on one property, all connected with this golf cart
train. We stop at each hotel—people getting on and
off. I love the international flavor of the Caribbean.
We aren't the only Americans here, but we're
definitely in the minority and I like it. Italians get on
from the casino hotel, all somehow looking
glamorous in their casual attire.

One year. The young widows' online group

warned that it would hit me in ways I didn't foresee. I'm not sad, more reflective. I know I can't stay busy forever. I can't travel indefinitely. That's sinking in on this trip.

I pick some flowers from the bushes as we walk from the restaurant to the beach for our walk back. We always choose to beach walk at night. All day I've wondered whether to mention the significance of today with the kids. I decide I will.

We walk, talk, sit. We remember Sean in our way, discuss how much he'd love being here, how much we miss him.

"Let's each say something special that we miss and put these flowers in the waves," I say. Not my idea...someone from the young widows' group had shared that with me before I left.

"I miss how he used to hold me on his shoulders," Bree says and tosses her flower into the wave.

"I miss how he used to read to me at night," Ben says. "He would have liked the moo restaurant."

"I miss his smile," I say before tossing my flower in the waves.

None of us say anything as we watch our flowers float on the water. I'm glad I'm honest with the kids. Yes, they're young, but they witnessed a horrific act a year ago. They've been on this journey with me every step of the way. They're young but not stupid. This is their life, their loss as much as mine. When they were born, I swore I'd never lie to them. This is how I've decided to handle it; perhaps I'll judge it as wrong later in life. For now, however, this feels right so I'm going with it. We acknowledge what we miss, remember Sean as we see fit, and are content being where we are. We're learning to be good as the Easton Three, a tight trio.

"Are we going to see your friend later?" Ben

asks, his hand in mine as we walk back to the hotel.

"Oh, I don't know. It's been a long day."

"We should go to the show," Bree says.

We do. I drink one too many mojitos. I try not to be sad. I see the Brazilian. I meet him later on the terrace. We dance.

When he kisses me, I hold on to him as if I never want to let go. I crave this feeling of being wanted, of not being alone in this moment, of being viewed only as a woman.

"Give up to grace. The ocean takes care of each wave 'til it gets to shore. You need more help than you know."
-- Rumi

Chapter Fifteen

The word widow is a hard label to carry. Since coming home from the Dominican Republic, I've encountered criticism for taking the kids there. It doesn't matter that we all had a great time or that I relaxed for the first time in twelve months.

"Spending recklessly," people say. "Aren't you worried about money?" They ask as if they're entitled to such information.

Well, you know what? It's not their damn money to worry about.

I say that, but the criticism is starting to whittle away at my fragile confidence. I already feel guilty for my time with the Brazilian. If people only knew about him...my, how they'd judge. *Look at the widow,* they'd say, *dancing with the Brazilian only one year after Sean's death. She must not have loved him. Look how she laughed, look how she danced.*

No, I'm not being fair. I don't know if that's what people would say. That's what I'm saying to *myself.* Guilt for having fun, for feeling alive while Sean has been reduced to ashes scattered on a mountainside, keeps me up all night. When people criticize my trips to my face, question when I'm going to write again or if I'm going to get a 'real' job, the guilt swells inside until I'm about to explode.

"How's the writing going?" They ask when they see me.

That's now become my most resented question.

"You're not a stay at home mom anymore, but you're acting like it. Must be nice," others comment. What am I supposed to say to that?

It's been a year; time is up for the mourning

period as far as most are concerned.

No one wants to see our pictures or hear about our trip to the Dominican Republic. Fine. We three have our own memories and that's all that matters.

I'm obsessing about the Brazilian. I see him in my dreams that usually end up as nightmares. I see Sean there, too. He's not really dead. He's alive, coming back, angry. How could I betray him?

How could he betray *me*? That's the counter argument, all in my mind. He's the one who left, not me. I have a right to live, don't I?

Guilt. I didn't anticipate this, and not just because of a stranger I met on vacation. This is guilt for being happy, for having fun, for getting a glimpse of what life could be like if I were to let the grief go.

I'm realizing that I haven't even begun to scratch the surface of this process. I feel like I'm unraveling, as if something inside me has finally broken open. I know intellectually that guilt is part of the grieving process, but I didn't understand the magnitude of what that meant. I've felt numb, sad, alone, confused, angry...but this guilt is unforgiving.

And why should I feel guilty for anything? I'm alive. I have two kids to raise and need to make sure their childhood isn't ruined because of their dad's suicide. I have a right to show them the world, to laugh, to dance, to have fun.

So why does it suddenly feel so wrong?

I'm falling apart on the inside—nightmares, shaking, more hair falling out, not eating—while trying to keep it together on the outside. My fierce grip that had held my seams together for a year has loosened and my stuffing is coming out.

I can't explain it, but something changed significantly for me in the Dominican Republic. I've been out of sorts since coming home, as if nothing around me fits anymore. Not my house, not the

mountain view, not the people I know, not my
routine that I'd clung to for the past year. I'm all out
of sorts.

I want to move, I've decided. I tell people this
and they look at me like I've sprouted horns. These
are the same people who were so sure I'd move
immediately after Sean died, now they're shocked that
I want to start over somewhere fresh.

I feel like I'm losing my mind.

The kids are going off for a weekend at Camp
Comfort, which is a grief camp for kids. I thought it
would be a good idea to go shortly after the one-year
mark, but now I'm not so sure.

For months now, I've been saying that the kids
need me to be with them all of the time; but as I'm
driving to Mount Evans to Camp Comfort, I realize
I'm terrified of coming back home alone.

The camp is full of cool looking cabins nestled
between towering pine trees. There's a pond and a zip
line. Camp counselors are a combination of volunteer
child psychologists and former campers who've come
back to be mentors. Both kids have said they feel like
they're the only ones whose dad has died—which
they are within their small circle. Ben has had friends
tell him to his face that he no longer has a dad so
can't talk about him. It's confusing for all of us. Here
they will meet other kids who have lost a parent. Kids
their own age. Good or bad, they'll realize they are
not unique.

Rational thought tells me that this is still a good
plan, that I'm doing the right thing. Victoria agrees.
She was also overjoyed to hear that I'd hooked up
with the Brazilian, says it's a good sign.

A sign of what, I don't know. Insanity maybe?

"You can't make me stay here," Bree says from
the backseat as we park. "I'm going home with you."

My hands are practically vibrating against the

steering wheel. "Bree, we've talked about this. You're going to stay here for a weekend with other kids. There will be games, campfires, zip lining, fishing...you're staying."

I'm irritated. Everything in my life is a fight. I can't even tell people about my trip to the Dominican Republic—which was a positive thing overall—without someone rolling their eyes over all my trips. *Fight, fight, fight.*

There are other women standing with children near the entrance. We're early. Bree has attached herself to my leg as we walk toward the group. Ben is clenching my hand. I hate that they're afraid, but I know I need to follow through with this.

I've learned to listen to my intuition above all else throughout this ordeal. It speaks louder than the fear. Right now it's telling me that this is the right thing to do.

I introduce myself to the other women. Yep, they're also widows. We speak quietly, bonded in a shared experience yet unsure how to act around our children who are all antsy about what's going on here.

The counselors are vibrant and welcoming. They show me the cabins. Bree and Ben will be split up. I know Bree has her anxiety, but she needs to do this. Her counselor is an older woman, a grief therapist in day-to-day life, so I know she's in good hands.

Ben, on the other hand, has already bonded with his male counselor who is talking to him about fishing and is excited about sleeping in a bunk bed.

Leaving is the hard part—especially when Bree has attached herself to my leg like a second skin.

"The best way to do this is to just go. She'll be fine once you're out of sight," her counselor tells me.

Guilt strangles me as I unwrap her fingers from my jeans. Tears blind me as I drive away with my last image of Bree being one of her screaming in the driveway.

I'm a horrible mother. That's all I think as I drive home. I'm screwing everything up. I'm spent a year traveling, acting like my life was the same by keeping a routine I thought was healthy, and now I'm abandoning my kids at a grief camp.

It's in the silence when the ghosts come. Nowhere to go. No project to work on. No escape. Suddenly the house echoes with all that once was and all that never will be.

Guilt consumes me.

Sean's family has nothing to do with us. *My fault.*

Most of my friends are gone. *My fault.*

The kids' friends are distancing themselves, being bullies in some cases. *My fault.*

I can't write. *My fault.*

I have no career, gave it up to stay home. Now what? *My fault.*

Sean is nothing but dust. *My fault.*

The kids don't have a daddy anymore. *My fault.*

My family is consumed with worry. *My fault.*

My kids' lives will forever be lacking. *My fault.*

I'm fucking everything up! *My fault.*

Insidious thoughts permeate my consciousness. In all of my thirty-eight years, I've never felt shame until now.

I feel ashamed for being a widow of someone who committed suicide. He didn't trust me enough to tell me his sadness...what does that say about me? The only reason the Brazilian was attracted to me was because he had no idea who I really was, what I'd done.

I feel shame for not being able to mend the bond with Sean's family who seem repulsed at the mere sight of me. I used to think I was a good person but...if I were a good person, why would all of this be happening in my life?

I'm letting the kids down. I forced them to go to Camp Comfort. Bree has anxiety issues yet I ripped her from my leg. I'm probably scarring them for life. I'm a rotten mother.

I'm an educated woman who once supported herself, who used to value independence, who had a plethora of friends. Now I'm alone in all ways that matter.

Loneliness. Until now I didn't fully understand that word.

I curl up on the floor, not having enough strength to get to a bed. I've lost everything that ever mattered to me. Sobs tear me apart, convulse through my gut, and rage through my throat until I no longer have a voice. Every doubt, every judgmental word I've heard, every fear is amplified.

That's how I feel in this moment. These are the thoughts that torment me like demons.

Even as I'm thinking these things, there's another voice inside me that says, "Stop lying, Amber. You know better than this. You are better than this. Don't surrender, stop thinking this way, it's wrong. Trust yourself. Fight the despair."

Fight, fight, fight.

* * * *

Sunday arrives and it's time to pick the kids up from camp. I'm there early as are the moms I met the other day. We chat, all nervous as to what kind of experience our children have had.

To our surprise, we're met with happy, laughing children who can't wait to introduce us to their new friends and tell us about their adventures. Well, who knew? The world didn't end, after all.

After a fun dinner with all of us, we meet in the main room where the kids have each prepared something to say about the parent they've lost. This is the sad part. All these children...all these sad stories...all ages...tragedy all around. But it's more than that. I feel the energy stir in the room. This is healing. They are holding each other's hands without adult guidance. They are speaking of their lost loved one openly in front of others who listen without judgment. This is an amazing scene to witness, all of these children bonded through grief who now know they are not alone.

We're all quiet as we walk outside and up the adjacent hill. It's beginning to rain. Each child has written a note to their deceased parent, a note they are not obligated to share with the living one. I have no idea what Bree or Ben has written. When Sean's name is called, they each walk to a small pine tree, say something I cannot hear, and tie their notes onto a branch with a ribbon. There it will stay. All around us are similar trees filled with notes from children to their parents who no longer walk the earth with them.

No one says anything as we walk to our individual vehicles with our children holding our hands. We are the living. That has value. We are not alone.

"Grief is a most peculiar thing; we're so helpless in the face of it. It's like a window that will simply open of its own accord. The room grows cold, and we can do nothing but shiver. But it opens a little less each time, and a little less; and one day we wonder what has become of it."
-- Arthur Golden, Memoirs of a Geisha

Chapter Sixteen
Autumn 2006

I'm home schooling Bree this school year, but now I'm prepared. She's enrolled in a part-time student program with our school district. Two days a week she takes classes like math, science, and drama at a middle school in Littleton. While she's in classes, I'm swimming at the recreation center, walking the stairs at Red Rocks Amphitheater, running errands, sitting in the park, or seeing Victoria. Bree and I are easing away from each other. Her anxiety attacks and sleepwalking are becoming few and far between. She's joined a volleyball team in addition to swimming. We're enjoying the home schooling, especially now that I have materials and a schedule, but know that it's temporary.

Ben is slowly rebounding from his learning setback. Slowly. He comes home sometimes in knots because he can't figure something out that used to be easy for him. His third grade teacher is much more understanding and willing to work with him than his second grade teacher had been.

I've started teaching writing to a group of home-schooled children every Friday morning. It's a group of about fifteen kids, ranging in grades from sixth to twelfth. It's basic stuff like essays, persuasive writing, and creative writing. I love it! I have a purpose. Lesson plans not only for Bree but also for the class.

I'm not writing, per se, but I've started carrying

around a few of the manuscripts I'd written or started to write before Sean died. Kiss Me Slowly and Riptide...both in serious need of revision. As I read them, I'm not sure I'll be able to write like that again. My brain feels filled with static more often than not. I carry them around with me anyway. Read them. Re-read them.

"How's the writing going?" Wow, that question is really getting old. I no longer answer people when they ask me this. I stare at them, not really caring what they think at this point.

I sob myself to sleep every night now that the kids have finally returned to their rooms. No one ever told me that the second year would be worse than the first. The numbness has worn off; the pain is inescapable.

My meetings with Victoria are more frequent and longer. The crack in my psyche that began in the Dominican Republic has grown. I've been ripped apart. Exposed. All my doubts about the marriage, about our battles to hold it together, about his abandonment, and my questions about how I'm making decisions come into play.

Victoria honors my choice not to go on medication. As an only parent, I don't want to be doped up in case the kids need me. She warns me that the grief process will only get worse before it gets better, but I feel I need to do this naturally. I make her a promise that if I ever feel that the bottom is dropping out—i.e. suicidal myself—that I'll let her do what she needs to do.

People don't realize that my self-confidence took a blow with Sean's death. My husband left me in the most final way imaginable. I feel beaten up. Everything I'd ever thought to be true has been proven a lie. I never thought Sean would kill himself. I also thought our love was true. I thought I could handle anything. Maybe I'd even been cocky.

Suicide knocks the cocky right out of a person. A year ago, last Fall, I'd told Victoria that I'd have my career back within three years, that I wouldn't be held back by any of this. Well, it's almost been a year and a half now and the closest I've come to working is teaching a group of home schooled kids and carrying old manuscripts around in my messenger bag.

You see, I don't have confidence to even try for anything more than that at this point. Every day I'm ravaged by sorrow. Family thinks it's depression, but this is grief. It's raw, merciless, deep, and scary. It's like I've been sucked under by a riptide and don't know which way is up.

Victoria says I need a mission statement for my life that doesn't involve the kids...or writing. I need a purpose that's not focused outward. What do I want for myself in the big scheme of things? Who am I beyond the roles of wife and mother?

Mission statement, huh? I'm reading books by Louise Hay and Dr. Wayne Dyer. I'm meditating, doing yoga, trying to calm my tumultuous thoughts.

My confidence comes and goes, as does my forward momentum. Victoria describes grief as a pendulum rather than a cycle. She says sometimes I'll be ahead and then swing backwards, eventually spending more and more time on the other side. I get glimpses of what "the other side of grief" is. I experienced it in the Dominican Republic, when I'm teaching Bree, and when the kids and I are doing something fun together.

I'll need to think about a personal mission statement...work it out in time.

We're busy with school and activities. I'm not coaching soccer anymore. We're going to a new team in the city with all new people. I'm learning that I can't escape the word widow, although I'd like to.

"What's your husband do?...Where's your husband?...Does Ben's father ever come to his games?"

"I'm a widow," I say over and over again. *I'm not divorced. Ben's dad used to be his coach. He's dead.*

"Oh, I'm so sorry. How'd he die?" That's what they ask. How.

I can't avoid the subject no matter how much I wish I could.

People advise to me lie about how Sean died so it's not so shocking for others to hear. There it is again...the implication of shame.

"You always look so sad," family says. "Snap out of it. It's been over a year now, you need to get on with your life."

I wish I could flick a switch and be out of this cycle. I wish I could write. I wish I had a confidante who'd come over for a glass of wine every now and then. I wish the kids' friends still wanted to come over instead of thinking of our house as the "place where that guy hung himself."

We go to hockey games about every other week. Perhaps one day I'll write an article about how hockey is saving our sanity. We go to Avalanche games. Scream. Cheer. Laugh. Chat with people around us. We have fun. Maybe it's not other people's idea of moving on or being healthy, but it works for us.

Fun is an amazing relief from grief. I highly recommend it.

I realize that many people don't understand us because they've never experienced anything like this at our age. By "this" I mean loss of a spouse. Perhaps they've lost a loved one—maybe even a parent later in life. Add suicide into the equation and people become uncomfortable. They also tend to forget that the kids and I saw him hanging there that day, witnessed the contortion of his face, heard his last breath after I'd cut him down, and tried to give him CPR. That's traumatic. The paramedics on the scene were even shocked that it happened with us in the house like that. The Victim's Advocate contacted me after the fact to say she was haunted by it and she'd seen many deaths. So why wouldn't we be affected?

I've had divorced friends tell me that I'm "lucky" that Sean is dead so I'm not in a perpetual battle like they are. They don't get it. I loved Sean— still do. The kids no longer have a father walking this earth. People see our trips, know that I'm able to stay at home, and think I must somehow be well off financially.

That's not the case. We had a safety net, that's true, but we're far from wealthy. I hear the comments, most of which are said to my face. I no longer care. That's the difference in me, too...I honestly don't care what the masses say about my choices. The Easton Three are still standing and that's all that matters. Being a mother gives me a purpose, gives me focus, gives me a reason to get out of bed every day.

The nightmares take a toll on me, both emotionally and physically. But then there are the other dreams...dreams where Sean is with me, alive, tanned, handsome, smiling, and telling me that he has faith in me. I never want to wake up from those dreams. Sometimes I wake up and swear my skin is warm from where he touched me. I love those dreams.

* * * *

For Sean's thirty-sixth birthday, I surprise the kids with a trip to Florida. They've been asking about his birthday, asking if we could do something to celebrate. I ask no one else's opinion about this decision. We go to Clearwater Beach.

Again, it's a good decision. While sitting on the

balcony of our hotel, we see dolphins leaping in the estuary. We're laughing together and exploring a new place. We're good on our own, maybe not perfect, perhaps more sad than not most days; but we're a tight trio.

On his birthday, we take a marine biology cruise in the estuary. Creatures of all kinds are pulled up in nets and passed around for us to examine before being dropped back into the water. Now this is the way to celebrate Sean's life! He loved the ocean. That evening, we walk on the beach and put notes to Sean in a balloon. The wind swoops it up and over the Gulf of Mexico.

I sit on the sand and watch the balloon ascend higher in the sky. I can't take credit for this idea; a woman on the young widows support group shared it with me.

No, I didn't want to be a single mom. I never anticipated being a widow. I'm probably making more mistakes than I realize, but we're still standing at the end of the day. We're still together...putting one foot in front of the other, sometimes falling backward, often scared. Time is a ridiculous measurement of healing. There is no timetable for grief. It rolls like the ocean waves, ebbs and flows like the tide. Some days are calm while others are like tsunamis.

This is our journey, no one else's. Our experience may be similar but not exactly like anyone else's. Other people's opinions of our process don't matter. They may hurt, but they don't count.

I still have a long way to go, but I finally wrote that mission statement for Victoria. I'll give it to her when we get home. Right now these words seem more like a fantasy and I understand I have a long way to go, but here it is:

"I intend to embrace creativity in all that I do. I intend to be a free-spirited, playful, humorous, highly successful, in-

demand, globe-trotting, independent woman who inspires others, and who is rooted in Divine energy."

It sounds happy to me, and I guess that's the point. That's what I want. It may need tweaking, but it's a beginning.

The kids are chasing sea birds along the beach. I imagine Sean would be proud of us. We're celebrating his life today, not lamenting his death. We're laughing in the sunshine, thinking of the future, remembering his goodness, and doing the best we can in the moment.

"There is a sacredness in tears. They are not the mark of weakness, but of power. They speak more eloquently than ten thousand tongues. They are the messengers of overwhelming grief, of deep contrition, and of unspeakable love."

--Washington Irving

Chapter Seventeen
May 29, 2007

Today we didn't run away. We're here, hiking up the mountain where we scattered Sean's ashes. We have the dogs, Taz and Dusty, and we're taking the long way around the mountain.

I haven't been here since the day of the funeral. It's time to go back.

With every step, I think of how far we've come...and how far we still need to go. People have told me that I need to move on, but I'm not sure what that means. I don't think even *they* know what that means. I realize that people around me simply want to see us happy, yet don't know how to articulate that so they say things like "move on" and "snap out of it" because they can't stand to see us hurting. Yes, their words have an adverse affect, but I realize that they don't know the right things to say.

I wanted to form a Survivors of Suicide group up here on the mountain, but the group's rules state that no one can lead a group until they have five years of recovery behind him/her. At first I didn't understand that, but now I do. It's been two years today and I'm not even a fraction of the way done with this process. The pendulum swings forward, then snaps me back when I least expect it.

I'm not sure why society has a timeline on grief—or why I bought into it at first. I measured myself against an impossible expectation. I'm glad I rejected that early on, even if it cost me a lot of relationships in the process. Today may be the two-year anniversary of that horrible day, but it feels like it's happening right now. The loss is sharp, vivid, and immediate.

Victoria, along with the numerous books I've read, says that the grief process usually takes between three to five years. Add trauma on top of that and it's an even longer journey. Sometimes I've wished I had that printed on a card that I could hand to someone when they start talking about me being stuck or measuring me to some ideal they have in their own minds.

The kids run around the hiking trail, pointing out chipmunks and rambling about mountain lions. The sun is blistering hot. We're walking through a part of the trail that's recovering from a forest fire. I see the towering black husks of trees; some have been cut down to prevent erosion. New trees sprout up between the old. Nature has a way of repairing itself and it takes many years to recover. It never grows back the same, but it's stunning in its newness.

Grief is like that—a devastation of all that once was with sprouts of new life appearing slowly but beautifully in between the ruins.

I miss Sean every day. I talk to him constantly in my dreams and, yes, in the closet. I keep finding love notes he tucked away for me. I'm not sure when he hid these because he'd always done romantic things like that even when we were dating. I remember going to the office, opening my briefcase, and finding a note about how much he'd miss me while I was at work. That's the kind of guy he was. Just the other day, a note fell out of one of my favorite novels...it said simply, *"I'll be thinking of you until I see you again...Love, Sean."*

I feel incredibly lucky to have been loved by a man like that. That's why this is so hard for me. I married a man I intended to grow old with. I loved him the day he died and I love him still. How do I move on from that? How do I reconcile the anger I still feel when I'm overwhelmed at being a single parent? How do I hate the addict when there was this good guy with the quick wink and easy smile who stashed love notes everywhere?

And the pendulum swings...back and forth between the emotions, good days to bad, happy memories transitioning to nightmares.

I'm supposed to go on a girls' trip to Cabo San Lucas in a few weeks and I don't want to go. Not really. I feel like I'm faking enthusiasm. All these years of pretending to be fine have worn me out. My zest for escape and immersing myself in forgetting is gone. All I want is solitude, time to face this head on, and figure out what this new normal truly means.

A year ago I was in the Dominican Republic drinking rum, dancing with a Brazilian, and doing my best to be far from here. I needed that then, but today we're visiting Sean on his quiet mountainside. It's time. We can't run forever. There comes a time when what we really need is to say this is what it is. Acceptance, I suppose. The manic go-go-go-do-do-do phase is behind me. My to-do list has been checked off. Now I'm filled with a numb acceptance, flashbacks of that horrible day, and the reality that I am a solo parent.

We reach Sean's boulder from the back of the mountain. I purposely took the long way so we could end our hike here. I packed snacks and brought Sean flowers. The kids take the dogs down the rock.

"Mom, look, there's something here for daddy," Ben says.

I jump down the main boulder to the outcropping where they stand. There on the side of the boulder facing the river is a plaque. It says "Sean

Michael Easton, November 6, 1970-May 29, 2005, beloved son, father, husband and friend. I miss you buddy, love, Dad."

I stare at it a minute before tracing my fingers over the words. I had no idea. I haven't seen his biological father since the funeral, haven't heard a word from his California relatives. This is something they did without including us. It's further proof of the division and the blame.

Bree retrieves the flowers I brought along from my backpack and puts them beneath the plaque.

"It's good that dad has a sign," she says.

"Yeah, it is." I accept the fact that his family will always have resentful feelings toward me. I wish it weren't so because of the kids, but there's not much more I can do.

I sit beneath a tree and stare down at the river below. Are some of his ashes here where I'm sitting or have they blown far down the mountain by now? Has he reached the stream? If so, how far has he traveled on the current? Has he reached the Gulf of Mexico yet?

"Sean, if you can hear me, can you see us? Are you walking with us, guiding us? Do you regret what you did? Are you helping us? Can you see how much we still love you?" I ask the questions silently as the kids walk around the boulders and the dogs run with them.

My wedding rings are back on my hand...my right hand. When I look down at them, I'm reminded that a beautiful blond boy who wrote love notes and taught me to look at the stars loved me. That matters.

I have a long way to go, I know. There is no timetable or rulebook for grief. There is no end to love. There is no shame in surviving the suicide of loved one.

I'm writing again, but only for myself. Tweaking. Testing. I'm surprised that the creativity is back. I've taken on a few freelance clients for business writing, but only a few. I don't trust myself yet. Like I've said, my confidence has taken a beating and writing is a profession that requires a lot of nerve.

"Mom, look!" Ben points at two hawks diving above us. They dip and dive backed by a flawless Colorado blue sky.

"I bet dad sees them every day," Bree says with such a confident smile I have no choice but to believe her.

"I bet he does." I pet Taz, our yellow lab, behind the ears and let the tears slip from my eyes. It's peaceful here. If nothing else, I hope Sean has found peace wherever he is now. I hope the demons that plagued him in life are silent.

Do I forgive him? Yes...sometimes. Do I still get angry? Hell, ya. I know that he did the best he could, though. Maybe it wasn't my best or my family's best or anyone else's idea of best, but he tried.

I'm trying. I'm progressing much more slowly than I anticipated, but maybe I'm like this burnt forest. A fire ravaged me, but I'm growing back at my own pace.

"Birds make great sky-circles of their freedom.
How do they learn it?
They fall and falling,
they're given wings."
-- *Rumi*

Fast Forward
May 29, 2013

Suicide leaves a stain on those who survive to mourn.

It took me a long time to get to a place where I could write this book. Healing isn't easy. I miss someone that the world tells me I should hate because he's committed suicide. As recently as a few months ago, a man I knew said I should change the kids' names to my maiden name because Sean didn't deserve a legacy. The judgment continues...only now I don't crumble when I hear it.

I've lost a lot of friends who couldn't deal with my sorrow or who didn't understand my process. I've had to let people go—including family members—who never understood that I'd never be the person I was before Sean's suicide, who couldn't process how grief affects someone, and who simply judged rather than loved.

I'm writing these words eight years to the day that Sean left this world. I've resumed my freelance writing and editing career, published three novels with more in progress, and have finally written this personal account of our journey. It took me five years to resume my career, and even then I started out with baby steps...a blog, a few articles, some editing projects. Kiss Me Slowly published via Siren-Bookstrand Publishing in November of 2011, which kicked off my novel writing career. Victoria had been right when she assured me that the creativity would return in time.

The kids are doing well; both are honor students, athletes, and normal teenagers. Bree returned to public school full-time in seventh grade. I view my decision to home school her as one of the best things I could have ever done, especially with the help of the Jefferson County school system's part-time student program. We needed the time-out and she returned to public school when she was ready. She and a group of other students from her high school are about to leave on an International Service trip to Greece where they'll work with orphans. Ben is looking more and more like his dad as he grows. I'm certain one day I'll turn around and see a living version of Sean standing in my living room. He's about to leave for to his grandpa's house for his annual summer trip to South Dakota.

Looking back, I know I made mistakes, most of them financial missteps or rash decisions like getting rid of our second car, but I forgive myself because I know I did the best I could in that moment. I learned to trust my instinct, to trust myself, and that proved the right move more often than not. My faith grew— faith in myself, faith in a Higher Power, and faith in life. Yes, I lost many friendships and family relationships changed over the past eight years; but I'm okay with all of that now. I'm different, therefore, so are the people I choose to know.

Dating...don't even get me started! I've heard comments such as *"you must have been hell to live with if your husband killed himself to get away from you"*..."maybe if he'd felt loved he wouldn't have resorted to suicide"..."you should probably lie about how your husband died, say it was an accident"..."you and your kids must be really damaged"*...and more absurd statement that would require another book to analyze.

I still miss Sean. I think of him almost every day. Now that the kids are older and off doing their

own thing more often than not, I wish he were here
for date nights. I wish he could see Bree graduate
high school and go off to college. I wish he could
cheer Ben on at lacrosse games. There will be big
moments in life where I'm certain he'll cross my
mind.

Grief does not go away, it evolves and changes
shape so that we learn to accept it as a part of us. It
deepens us, and in its way, strengthens us.

In both my Survivors of Suicide and Young
Widows Bulletin Board groups, they speak of active
grieving versus passive grieving. The first is the raw,
brutal, nasty emotional ride that rips you up and
tosses you around. The second is a gentler, almost
peaceful missing of someone you wish still walked
beside you.

Now, eight years later, do I forgive Sean for his
suicide, for his struggles during our marriage?
Sometimes, yes; sometimes, no. It truly depends on
the day and the circumstance. That's the truth of it.
My truth. My normal. When I'm alone dealing with
teenage drama, I wish I could say something like
"don't make me tell your dad about this." Knowing
that I don't have that option—and neither do the
kids—aggravates me at times. Mostly, though, I'm sad
for Sean because he is missing out on knowing the
children he loved.

I am honest with the kids about his struggle
with alcoholism. When they ask about their dad, I tell
them what they need to know. After all, they were
with me that day when we found him hanging, they've
walked with me through this process, and they
deserve my honesty.

I've done the best that I could within the
mindset that I had at the time. There were moments
when despair prevented me from thinking straight,
even when I appeared normal and 'together' on the

outside. I'd go so far to say that I lost myself in despair for a few years. But I survived. That's what I want to convey...there *is* another side to grief. There are new beginnings for all of us.

Yes, there's happiness and a lot of laughter—even after falling apart or maybe because of it. I know darkness now. I know the depths I can fall. I also know how high I can soar and how amazing joy is.

We're good, the three of us Eastons. I feel like I have finally reclaimed my life, my career, myself. I laugh more than I cry these days, which says a lot when I cried every night for years. I've taken up belly dancing with a group of wonderful women, joined a hiking club to meet new people, and am thinking of relocating to the ocean once both kids have graduated high school.

Victoria's mission statement assignment is pinned to the bulletin board next to my desk, reminding me that I have a life of my own to live.

I've learned a lot about myself throughout this journey. I've learned that I'm much stronger than I ever thought possible. I've learned that not everyone in my life is equipped to handle such darkness, but that's okay. This has been my journey, not theirs.

If I can presume to give any advice at this point—I hate the word *advice*—let me say that, if you're the one experiencing the loss, roll with all the emotions, reject the idea of shame people may try to cast upon you, and know that you'll eventually find peace. If you're the support system for someone who's experienced loss, then all you need to do is be the person who listens to the same story a thousand times, who holds the hand, who shows up months later, and who stays all the way through no matter what.

I've learned that love doesn't end with death

and that I don't need to justify that to anyone. The vows "til death do us part" fail to acknowledge that love is infinite. I've also learned not to take anything for granted because it could all come shattering to an end at any moment.

Victoria's description of grief as a pendulum that swings back and forth through the stages—sometimes spending more time forward, which tricks you into thinking it's over, and then yanks you backward—was accurate. Eventually, however, the pendulum swings you over the threshold to 'the other side' filled with new beginnings, hope, and happiness.

"What's past is prologue, and the world awaits."
-- Jo Mantchev, Eyes Like Stars

The Easton Three—with buddies Dusty and Carl—
Christmas 2012

About the Author

Amber Lea Easton is a multi-published author of both nonfiction and fiction. She spent years working in journalism and advertising with a brief detour into the financial sector. In addition to this nonfiction book, Free Fall, she has three published romantic suspense novels—Kiss Me Slowly, Riptide, and Reckless Endangerment—with a fourth, Dancing Barefoot, due to release later in 2013.

Easton is also an editor and speaker. Links to radio interviews can be located on her website, http://amberleaeaston.com, and her videos about romance writing have been showcased internationally on the Writers and Authors television network.

Easton currently lives with her two teenagers in the Colorado Rocky Mountains. She gives thanks daily for the view outside her window and healthy children. As long as she's writing, she considers herself to be simply "a lucky lady liv'n the dream."

http://www.amberleaeaston.com

http://www.facebook.com/AuthorAmberLeaEaston

Survivors of Suicide's website:
http://www.survivorsofsuicide.com

Young Widows Bulletin Board:
http://www.ywbb.org/chaptertwo.shtml

CPSIA information can be obtained
at www.ICGtesting.com
Printed in the USA
LVHW071037130119
603753LV00001B/16/P

* 9 7 8 0 6 1 5 8 7 9 5 4 3 *